THE WORKINGS OF DIASPORA

Critical Africana Studies: African, African American, and Caribbean Interdisciplinary and Intersectional Studies

The Critical Africana Studies book series features scholarship within the emerging field of Africana studies, which encompasses such disciplines as African studies, African diasporan studies, African American studies, Afro-American studies, Afro-Asian studies, Afro-European studies, Afro-Islamic studies, Afro-Jewish studies, Afro-Latino studies, Afro-Native American studies, Caribbean studies, Pan-African studies, Black British studies and, of course, Black studies. The Critical Africana Studies book series directly responds to the heightened demand for monographs and edited volumes that innovatively explore Africa and its diaspora employing cutting-edge critical, interdisciplinary, and intersectional theory and methods.

Recent Titles in the Series

The Workings of Diaspora: Jamaican Maroons and the Claims to Sovereignty, By Mario Nisbett

Race, Identity, and Privilege from the US to the Congo, By Brenda F. Berrian

Ama Mazama: The Ogunic Presence in Africology, By Molefi Kete Asante

The Afrocentric Pan Africanist Vision: Afrocentric Essays, By Molefi Kete Asante

Branches of Asanteism, By Abdul Karim Bangura

Transcendence and the Africana Literary Enterprise, Edited by Christel N. Temple and foreword by Molefi Kete Asante

Strategies for Success among African-Americans and Afro-Caribbeans: Overachieve, Be Cheerful, or Confront, By Chrystal Y. Grey and Thomas Janoski

Rastafari Reasoning and the RastaWoman: Gender Constructions in the Shaping of Rastafari Livity, By Jeanne Christensen

Conceptual Aphasia in Black: Displacing Racial Formation, Edited by P. Khalil Saucier and Tryon P. Woods

THE WORKINGS OF DIASPORA

Jamaican Maroons and the Claims to Sovereignty

Mario Nisbett

LEXINGTON BOOKS

Lanham • Boulder • New York • London

Published by Lexington Books
An imprint of The Rowman & Littlefield Publishing Group, Inc.
4501 Forbes Boulevard, Suite 200, Lanham, Maryland 20706
www.rowman.com

86-90 Paul Street, London EC2A 4NE

Parts of introduction and chapters 1, 3, and 4 were previously published in *Symbolism* and used with permission.

Mario Nisbett, "African Diasporic Traditional Symbols and Claims"; in: Rüdiger Ahrens, Florian Kläger, Keith A. Sandiford and Klaus Stierstorfer (eds.) of *Symbolism: An International Annual of Critical Aesthetics, Volume 16*, Berlin, Germany: De Gruyter, 2016, pp. 117–138.

Mario Nisbett, "Claiming Asante: The Akan Origins of Jamaican Maroons," in *The Asante World (17–21st Century)*, eds. Edmund Abaka and Kwame Osei Kwarteng (New York: Routledge, 2021), 255–277.

Mario Nisbett, "Defining and Utilizing Diaspora: Towards a Path to African Post-Development," *Contemporary Journal of African Studies* 8, Nos. 1 & 2 (2021).

British Library Cataloguing in Publication Information Available

Library of Congress Cataloging-in-Publication Data

Names: Nisbett, Mario, 1975- author.
Title: The workings of diaspora : jamaican maroons and the claims to sovereignty / Mario Nisbett.
Other titles: Workings of diaspora in Jamaican Maroon communities
Description: Lanham : Lexington Books, [2021] | Series: Critical africana studies | Includes bibliographical references and index.
Identifiers: LCCN 2021038967 (print) | LCCN 2021038968 (ebook) | ISBN 9781793613882 (cloth) | ISBN 9781793613905 (paper) | ISBN 9781793613899 (ebook)
Subjects: LCSH: Maroons—Jamaica—Ethnic identity. | Maroons—Jamaica—Social life and customs. | Jamaica—Social life and customs. | African diaspora—Social conditions.
Classification: LCC F1896.B53 N57 2021 (print) | LCC F1896.B53 (ebook) | DDC 305.896/07292—dc23
LC record available at https://lccn.loc.gov/2021038967
LC ebook record available at https://lccn.loc.gov/2021038968

Contents

Acknowledgments

THE JOURNEY OF WRITING this book (which began as a dissertation) would not have been possible without the support and encouragement of many people, communities, and institutions. Most importantly, I would like to thank my family. I cannot express in words the significance of the unwavering support in this endeavor from my parents, Ernest and Merriss Nisbett. Indeed, I thank my wife, Rosemary Appoh-Nisbett, too, for all of her support and encouragement. Also, I greatly appreciate the guidance and mentorship of Percy Hintzen, who continues to inspire me with his thought-provoking understanding and ideas about our world. Moreover, I would like to thank G. Ugo Nwokeji for his encouragement and support as well.

I sincerely appreciate the support in one way or another from community members in Accompong Town, Charles Town, Moore Town, and Scot's Hall. However, it was in Accompong Town of the Maroon communities I spent most of my time. So, it is to them I owe the most gratitude.

I would like to thank loved ones, friends, colleagues, and students who directly assisted me in transforming the dissertation into a book. They were key in helping me with the revising and developing of the work. These individuals are Evelyn Adjandeh, Yaw Adjei-Gyamfi, Michael Agbo, Rosemary Appoh-Nisbett, Rita Y. Bansah, Natasha Bynoe, Andre Daniel, James Essilfie, Justin Gomer, Derick Hendricks, Percy Hintzen, Amartey Rashid Laryea, Chika Mba, Stephen Mensah, Merger Nisbett-Ottley, Tony Talburt, Michael Thomas, and Moussa Traore. I am as well grateful in many ways for the contribution of the following institutions: The African Caribbean Institute of Jamaica, Butler Library (at Columbia University), Cape Coast Dungeon-Castle (Ghana),

Clark University, Fort Amsterdam (Ghana), the Jamaica National Heritage Trust, Lexington Books, the Manhyia Palace (Ghana), the National Archives of Jamaica, the National Library of Jamaica, the Smithsonian Institution, the Social Development Commission (Jamaica), Susquehanna University (including a grant supporting my latter research in Jamaica), UC Berkeley (especially the Department of African American Studies and the Center for African Studies), University of Cape Coast, University of Ghana, and the University of the West Indies, Mona Campus (including the Sir Arthur Lewis Institute of Social and Economic Studies and the Main Library). Their support was instrumental in the completion of the manuscript.

Overall, I am thankful for the direct or indirect support of other loved ones, friends, colleagues, and students, which include Edmund Abaka, Robert Allen, Alexia Anderson, Kobina Nhyira Appoh-Nisbett, Kwame Ato Asiedu, Johannis Aziz, Isaac Barnard, Carol Barnett, Lia Bascomb, La Toya Beck, Peter Bembeir, Charisse Burden-Stelly, Horace Campbell, Harris Cawley, James Chambers, Oral Chambers, Patanjali Chary, Eric Cleveland, Ayanna Cole, Larissa Cole, Venetta Cole, Rob Connell, Catilda Connor, Melville Currie, Sarah Daniels, Abraham Amoah Danquah, Kelley Deetz, Hubert Devonish, Mamadou Diouf, Marcia Douglas, Clive Downer, J. Finley, Constant Foster, Ikamellia Foster, Mjiba Frehiwot, Hardy Frye, Millicent Graham, Horace Grant, Shauntay Grant, Rashida Hanif, Sharon Harris, Charles Henry, Lindsey Herbert, Abraham Hodey, Dorcie Huggins, George Huggins, Jerry Howard, Ann-Marie Hutchinson, Stephanie Jackson, Bernard Jankee, Henrietta Jones, Jasminder Kaur, Malgorzata Kurjanska, Leece Lee, Kerima Lewis, Marcia Lobban-Martin, Ameer Loggins, Frank Lumsden, Selina Makana, Leonora Maloney, Rohan Maloney, Sidney Maloney, Vincia Maloney, Bryan Mason, Michael McGee, Dominique McIndoe, Kim McNair, Carmen Mitchell, Courtney Morales, Alex Moulton, Na'ilah Nasir, Akasemi Newsome, Kwame Nimako, Irene Odotei, Ernestina Ohenewaah, Amaka Ohia, Ianna Owens, Keerthi Potluri, Noel Prehay, Leigh Raiford, Ankur Rastogi, Hansley Reid, Lance Ricketts, Alaine Rowe, Ann-Marie Rowe, Garfield Rowe, Jerel Rowe, Kevin Rowe, Lawrence Rowe, Patrice Rowe, Shelly-Ann Rowe, Norma Rowe-Edwards, Maxine Royston, Reggie Royston, Shelby Russell, Emmanuel Saboro, Alisa Sanchez, Keith Sandiford, Kwaku Sarpong, David Scott, Stephen Small, Kathy Smith, Juliana Sofoa, Wallace Sterling, Krystal Strong, Ula Taylor, Narh Tei-Kumadoe, Christel Temple, Matthew Valades, Kenrick Wallace, Sheldon Wallace, Oral White, Laurie Wilkie, Ferron Williams, Gabrielle Williams, Ron Williams, Veta Williams, Alex J. Wilson, Amy Wolfson, Tyshan Wright, and Wilson Yayoh.

Introduction

> One of the most important things for us, Maroons, is to maintain our African traditions.
>
> —Colonel Ferron Williams of Accompong Town Maroon Community[1]

The Maroons

JAMAICAN MAROON communities, the oldest independent polities in the Caribbean, were established by escapees from Spanish and British slave-holding societies during the sixteenth, seventeenth, and eighteenth centuries.[2] The existence of these Maroon communities of the African Diaspora has clearly disproved a particular European modernist view of "black" peoples by invalidating the pernicious idea of Africans and their descendants as being complacent in slavery and unable to govern themselves.

The rise of Maroon communities all over the Western Hemisphere during the Transatlantic slavery era was significant. The sheer proliferation and ubiquity of these societies were astonishing. The emergence of autonomous zones in every region of all colonial possessions made it impossible for the European imperialists to claim complete territorial integrity of their domains in the Americas. In fact, many such societies antedated and have outlasted the rule of some of the Western colonial powers in the "New World." They have constituted an important part of African Diaspora resistance to the European colonial regimes. These communities, especially the most firmly established ones, such as the Jamaican Maroons, are legacies of black political resistance in the face of expanding European hegemony in the Western Hemisphere.

However, in contemporary times, the significance of the Maroons has been mainly relegated to the annals of histories of African resistance to slavery. This particular point was expressed by present-day Jamaican Maroon leaders, such as Frank Lumsden (2004–2015) and Wallace Sterling (1995–present), who lament that most scholars have focused on the Maroons of the past and neglected the contemporary ones. Now that there exist many black independent Caribbean states, Maroons are generally seen as politically unimportant to the current contributions to the African Diaspora.

Nevertheless, Maroons (phenomenologically) continue to recognize their own importance to African Diaspora politics. The enduring diasporic significance in Maroon communities is seen through their claimed African-derived socio-political organization, communal lands, relationship with food, belief systems, storytelling, language, material culture, and traditional music, dance, and drumming. The Jamaican Maroons represent and display their diasporic relevance to the public in texts, oral histories, ceremonies, images, landmarks, architecture, and monuments. Locally, through Grandy Nanny, the only national heroine and the most famous of all female Maroon leaders, the importance of the Maroon communities is kept alive and well. Internationally, one of these communities, Moore Town, has been recently proclaimed by UNESCO as a site representing the Masterpiece of the Oral and Intangible Heritage of Humanity, giving credit to the long-lived legacy of Maroons' independence and freedom-fighting spirit as a people of African descent.[3]

As this book argues, Maroons are still contributing to the significance of African Diaspora politics. As in the past, Maroon communities in modern times resist prevailing political thought on acceptable forms of political organizing. Maroons' independence is about not only the past but also the relentless struggle in the post-colonial era, which in many ways still restricts freedoms. Indeed, there is something to be said about the limits of self-determination in what Sabelo J. Ndlovu-Gatsheni, drawing on Gayatri C. Spivak, refers to as a "post-colonial era" in a "neo-colonized world," in which formerly colonized peoples still find themselves entangled.[4] Members of Maroon communities, through the positioning of their "uniqueness," continue to forge a path of independence. As people of African descent, Jamaican Maroons are in full pursuit of sovereignty in this neo-colonial global order.

In the twenty-first century, Maroon communities continue to contribute to the understanding of the New World diasporic experience and aspirations. Maroons created and continue to sustain distinctive and dynamic political formations that, though subtle, challenge the hegemonic societies they seceded from. As diasporic communities, modern-day Jamaican Maroon communities are constituted through 1) their central societal values of freedom; 2) being living examples of reciprocal relations through communal-held lands and environmental spaces; 3) community linkages that transcend the state; 4) extensive transnational networks; and 5) most recently, a mobile population.

Engaging the past, the present, and visions of the future, *The Workings of Diaspora: Jamaican Maroons and the Claims to Sovereignty* makes an intervention that firmly links the lived experience of Jamaican Maroons to the African Diaspora and its politics. In so doing, this interdisciplinary undertaking interrogates the conceptualization of Diaspora but mainly emphasizes the word's usage. It shows that an examination of Jamaican Maroon communities, and particularly their socio-political development, can further highlight the significance of the African Diaspora as an analytical device. It demonstrates how Jamaican Maroons can inform others about resisting abjection—as in denial of full humanity—in claiming African origin and developing collective consciousness in order to affirm black humanity. It establishes that Jamaican Maroon communities are still relevant and engage the African Diaspora in working to improve black standing and reinforce assertions of sovereignty.

The Workings of Diaspora explores in detail the emergence and development of Jamaican Maroons in the next chapter. This introduction focuses on the conceptualization of Diaspora, thus providing the context to thoroughly examine the Jamaican Maroons' engagement with the African Diaspora and its politics.

The African Diaspora

The concept of Diaspora is being used with increasing sophistication and wider application in recent times. This notion has been appropriated for an ever-growing number of communities, cultures, and populations for whom it had not been used before to explain the intricacies of their condition.

The increasingly popular use of the term "Diaspora" has incited a scholarly debate about its definition. Some academics, such as Brent Hayes Edwards and Darlene Clark Hine, have reasonable concerns about the conceptualization of the notion, with Khachig Tölölyan going as far to say that it is "in danger of becoming promiscuously capacious."[5] As a category, it can include adjacent phenomena such as globality, migrancy, post-coloniality, and transnationality.[6] For this reason, scholars such as Kim Butler, James Clifford, and Thomas Faist have argued that the term has no clear definition.[7] Evelyn Hu-DeHart, perhaps prematurely, believes that Diaspora "has lost much utility for careful and precise academic analysis" and that "it is time to move on and embrace newer terms and concepts."[8]

It may not be possible to precisely define Diaspora, but I find it fruitful to explore the specific Diaspora that is the African Diaspora, which is a more distinctive term. The African Diaspora is different from other Diasporas in that it may refer to peoples of African descent in and from various communities that may also be a part of other Diasporas: religious (such as Muslim), ethnic (such as Yoruba), and national (such as Nigerian or Jamaican). The African Diaspora may be conceptualized differently from a Ghanaian (or Gold Coast) Diaspora or an Akan Diaspora, although they may overlap in significant ways. These definitions ought to accept Earl Lewis's idea of overlapping Diasporas without losing the sense of conceptualizing a particular one.[9]

Here I am proposing an additional definition to the number of other accepted conceptualizations of the African Diaspora: that it is the circumstance of peoples regarded to be outside of their "homeland" and deemed to be of African origin who, fostering a type of unity, having to confront various forms of oppression. In other words, and more strictly, the African Diaspora is the condition that produces the shared consciousness of a sameness rooted in the idea of common African origin and based on a common experience of black abjection. We find the three major principles embedded in this definition—collective consciousness, common origin, and abjection—implicitly and explicitly expressed in the popular and well-established attempts to conceptualize the African Diaspora.

Diasporic Framework and Framing

A diasporic framework was already in use before the specific concept of African Diaspora gained its present prevalence. Starting in the early nineteenth century, this framework was evident in the challenges to the discursive exclusion of black peoples from enlightened humanity. Indeed, the historian George Shepperson referred to the diasporic framing as a challenge to influential post-Enlightenment figures such as G. W. R. Hegel, who said in his famous lectures on history in Berlin that Africa (and, in effect, peoples of African descent) had "no historical part of the World . . . no movement or development to exhibit" and was "only on the threshold of the World's History."[10] Since then, prominent educators and intellectuals such as Mary McLeod Bethune, Edward Wilmot Blyden, W. E. B. Du Bois, and Amy Jacques Garvey have used a diasporic framework to express ideas that bring greater awareness of black abjection and oppose its harmful effects. A diasporic framing, prior to the use of the word "Diaspora," was used to stress the humanity of black peoples who have been shut out from the world by a vast "veil."[11]

Beginning in the 1950s, the term "African Diaspora" has been systematically applied to the black historical experience. From that time, there have been increasing attempts at conceptual clarity. Notions of a common experience of oppression, common origin, and shared solidarity have been highlighted.

Many of the scholarly efforts to define the African Diaspora have fundamental elements in common. The historian Joseph Harris, one of the earliest theorists of the African Diaspora, has had perhaps the most significant impact on the development of African Diaspora studies and its conceptualization. Harris sees Diaspora as having the following characteristics: "[1] Collective memories and myths about Africa as the homeland or place of origin; [2] a tradition of a physical and psychological return; [3] a common socioeconomic condition; [4] a transnational network; and [5] a sustained resistance to Africans' presence abroad and an affirmation of their human rights."[12] Supporting my argument, these elements can be considered common conditions that connect diverse peoples based on the idea of common origin, a collective consciousness of sameness, and a shared experience of abjection (causing the conditions that lead to the drive for the "affirmation of their human rights").

More recently, Colin Palmer, following in the tradition of Harris, presents Diaspora as imaginary and symbolic communities and political constructs having the following characteristics:

> [1] Regardless of their location, members of a Diaspora share an emotional attachment to their ancestral land, [2] are cognizant of their dispersal and, [3] if conditions warrant, of their oppression and alienation in the countries in which they reside. [4] Members of diasporic communities also tend to possess a sense of "racial," ethnic, or religious identity that transcends geographic boundaries, [5] to share broad cultural similarities, and [6] sometimes to articulate a desire to return to their original homeland.[13]

Thus, Palmer, like Harris, defines Diaspora as (a) a common experience of oppression and alienation, (b) rooted in a sense of collective consciousness, and (c) oriented toward a notion of common origin.

Moreover, Paul Zeleza, in his "The Challenges of Studying the African Diasporas," observes that Diaspora can be seen simultaneously as "a process, a condition and a discourse."[14] In his conceptualization, he highlights the significance of group consciousness, marginalization, self-affirmation, belonging, origin, and real and imagined genealogies. These elements can again be considered as common conditions that connect a diverse set of peoples based on the idea of common origin, collective consciousness of sameness, and shared experience of exclusion.

Diasporic Critical Practice

It is important to recognize these endeavors at defining Diaspora as an effort to understand not only what Diaspora is but also what it does: to comprehend it not in a literal sense but as a critical practice. The term "Diaspora," as Stuart Hall suggests, can be used in a literal or "closed" way to describe peoples who have been dispersed from their "countries of origin" but who attempt to maintain links with the past through endeavors to preserve their traditions, "seeking eventually to return to the homeland—the true 'home' of their culture—from which they have been separated."[15] However, Hall also proposes what could be called a more "open" or critical and more complex sense in which Diaspora could be seen:

> Diaspora also refers to the scattering and dispersal of peoples who will never literally be able to return to the places from which they came; who have to make some kind of difficult "settlement" with the new, often oppressive, cultures with which they were forced into contact; and who have succeeded in remaking themselves and fashioning new kinds of cultural identity by, consciously or unconsciously, drawing on more than one cultural *repertoire*. These are people who, as Salman Rushdie wrote in his essay in *Imaginary Homelands*, "having been borne across the world . . . are translated men (and women)" (Rushdie, 1991, p. 17). . . . They speak from the "in-between" of different cultures, always unsettling the assumptions of one culture from the perspective of another, and thus finding ways of being both the same as and at the same time different from the others among whom they live (Bhabha 1994).[16]

This critical—rather than literal—usage of Diaspora opens up many possibilities and complicates the literal interpretation. One of these possibilities is how it opens ways to understand the critical view of Diaspora as a metaphor to the literal interpretation. As an alternative to a literal interpretation, Percy Hintzen argues that Diaspora, when "transferred as a signification of the Black social reality, served as a powerful metaphor to publicize the even more devastating, brutal, and pervasive violence that constituted the common history of colonialism and slavery."[17] Critically, the African Diaspora in comparison to the well acknowledged Jewish diasporic condition brings to light what might have not been recognized in the experience of displacement, exclusion, and sharing of consciousness of black peoples.

The critical view also makes it possible to fully engage the lived experience of diasporic communities in order to better understand the workings of the concept itself. It allows for the opportunity to appreciate various black peoples, phenomenologically distinctive engagement with the African Diaspora.[18]

The critical understanding reveals that the African Diaspora in its workings is significantly about resistance. It is resistance to abjection in engaging African origin and collective consciousness in advancing black standing.

In this view, the critical practice of the African Diaspora can be understood as utterances or acts that critique the Othering of African-descended peoples. The critical practice of Diaspora is manifest in expressive forms. Indeed, critical practice is the mode of expression out of which Diaspora is articulated (enunciated and productive of linkages based on sameness across difference). In particular, what is phenomenologically expressed is related to abjection, common origin, and collective consciousness.

These central principles contribute to the understanding of Diaspora as a critical practice, which I conceive here as forms of expression out of which Diaspora may be articulated or made discernible. These three principles that could be seen as critical practice, all conditions of the African Diaspora, are the common experience of black abjection, organized around notions of common African origin, and constituted by forms of universal black consciousness.

The first core principle of abjection is significant in the condition that produces the African Diaspora. Hence, any and all efforts to exclude groupings of human beings from partial or full rights of humanity in any form are abjection.[19] In particular, black abjection results from the Europeans' efforts to dehumanize the African, whom they racialized as black. Fundamentally, it is what Africans are resisting and gives further impetus to engaging the idea of origin (see chapter two for elaboration of abjection).

In resisting black abjection, another central element of the concept of African Diaspora is the idea of common African origin. All peoples of African descent are linked to the notion of "Africa." One cannot speak of the African Diaspora without engaging this central idea. In fact, ideas of origin in a particular homeland are argued to be the most significant attributes of diasporic peoples. Even in disavowing origin, it is still engaged. It is important to note: this idea of common origin in Africa must be understood as a strategic reaction of peoples who are racialized as "black" seeking home and belonging (see chapter three for elaboration of origin).

Influenced by the notion of origin, the final core principle of the African Diaspora is the idea of a collective consciousness of sameness. Collective consciousness is produced out of a mutual awareness of shared circumstances and experiences. It is mutual recognition of sameness across difference (see chapter four for elaboration of collective consciousness).

Diasporic Articulation

In the engagement of these core elements—abjection, origin, and collective consciousness—of the African Diaspora, the understanding of articulation is essential. The significance of articulation has been argued by Stuart Hall, Brent Hayes Edwards, and other scholars.

Articulation is a process of not only creating but also re-creating enunciations and linkages among groupings of people.[20] In this instance, it is articulation as it applies to peoples of African descent in Africa and throughout the world. As Lawrence Grossberg argues about Hall's understanding of the concept, articulation is defined and could be understood in the following way:

> In England, the term has a nice double meaning because "articulate" means to utter, to speak forth, to be articulate. It carries that sense of language-ing, of expressing, etc. But we also speak of an "articulated" lorry [truck]: a lorry where the front (cab) and back (trailer) can, but need not necessarily, be connected to one another. The two parts are connected to each other, but through a specific linkage, that can be broken. An articulation is thus the form of the connection that *can* make a unity of two different elements, under certain conditions. It is a linkage which is not necessary, determined, absolute and essential for all time. You have to ask, under what circumstances *can* a connection be forged or made? So the so-called "unity" of a discourse is really the articulation of different, distinct elements which can be rearticulated in different ways because they have no necessary "belongingness." The "unity" which matters is a linkage between that articulated discourse and the social forces with which it can, under certain historical conditions, but need not necessarily, be connected. Thus, a theory of articulation is both a way of understanding how ideological elements come, under certain conditions, to cohere together within a discourse, and a way of asking how they do or do not become articulated at specific conjunctures, to certain political subjects.[21]

Articulation is a way of understanding dynamic, complex, and fluid relations. It is in this setting that Edwards introduces the term *décalage*, which refers to gaps that make linking (articulation), de-linking (dis-articulation), and re-linking (re-articulation) possible among groupings of black peoples.[22] In this process, articulation is the bringing of relations into meaningful coherence. As John Fiske affirms, Hall's "double use of the concept of articulation (both speaking [sense 1] and [flexible] linking [sense 2]) is central in his theorizing."[23] This view of articulation refuses to allow meaning any fixity, but "is insistent that meanings *are* made, *are* held in place and *are* used in particular if temporary conditions."[24] Articulation can be understood as a way of characterizing a social relation without becoming reductionist and essentialist.[25]

Articulation gives one a way to understand the subject of analysis. As Jennifer Slack asserts, articulation works as a means of thinking through "the structures of what we know as a play of correspondences, non-correspondences and contradictions, as fragments in the constitution of what we take to be unities."[26]

The analytic focus on articulation allows for understanding the (often phenomenological) claims to unity of diverse peoples who are conceptualized as black. Hall rightly asserts that when one is speaking of black cultures, one cannot speak for long, with any exactness, about a history of one people or experience.[27] Indeed, cultures of black peoples are not "fixed essences that lie unchanged and that already existed, transcending place, time, history and culture."[28] The histories of black cultures, as Hall suggests, "have their real, material and symbolic effects" that "continue to speak to us," but they "no longer address us as a simple, factual 'past,' since our relation to it, like the child's relation to the mother, is always-already 'after the break.' It is always constructed through memory, fantasy, narrative and myth."[29] The cultures of black peoples come from many different sites and, like everything historical, they constantly undergo change and transformation.[30]

Articulation creates the space for understanding the connections of different African-descended cultures and identities with one another. As Edwards asserts, "articulation offers the means to account for the diversity of Black 'takes' on the very concept of Diaspora."[31] Indeed, each community phenomenologically has a different engagement with the Diaspora. Hence, articulation becomes a critical practice of thinking about unity in difference. Articulation recognizes that black peoples have been and continue to be a set of multiple and constantly shifting cultures and identities that are not easily categorized but can still be uttered and linked. Articulation becomes central in the idea of a black "sameness" across difference.

Diasporic Politics

Earlier, I argued that the African Diaspora is constituted of three factors, all embedded in its various definitions: the common experience of abjection, the notion of common African origin, and a collective consciousness of sameness. As critical practice and articulation, Diaspora is engaged with each of these. It is this engagement that produces the "politics of Diaspora," or the political expressions of a universal black subjecthood that resist the narratives of Othering. Diaspora politics is engaged in a quest for dignity, equality, justice, and rights. The politics of Diaspora is a struggle for recognition of the humanity of the African subject. The politics, a product of the recognition of sameness, produces new possibilities and new forms of consciousness about the African self. It has the potential to reveal African humanity fully and serves as the basis for black liberation.

Diasporic Formation: Culture, Identity, and Race

The African Diaspora (as well as its elemental components) and its engagement with culture, identity, and race ought to be not essentialized. It is important to examine diasporic peoples, as Aisha Khan rightly echoes, "as part of cultures rather than as possessors of culture."[32] In a similar vein, identity/identities ought to be considered not in a rigid manner but more as a form of consciousness.[33]

Notably, the association between blackness and Africa is a problematic product of European racial thinking. I view race here to be a social construct that has no biological basis and, following Michael Omi and Howard Winant, is "at best imprecise and at worst completely arbitrary."[34] It is crucial to understand that, in its critical practice and articulation, the African Diaspora is not a subscription to an essentialist racial agenda. However, it does strategically engage it because of its concrete and destructive effects.

Various cultures, identities, or racial categories engage the African Diaspora, and it is not inherent, but these notions become diasporic. It can be said that African diasporic groups exist phenomenologically.[35] Therefore, it is best to explore the African Diaspora from the inside as an experience.[36] In Khan's appeal, it is best to see the African Diaspora "as a condition of possibility, as a means to an end that is open and contingent rather than predictive, proving a point."[37]

Diasporic Interdisciplinarity

The African Diaspora—as critical practice, articulation, and politics—is significantly at the heart of the interdisciplinary field of African Diaspora studies. Hence, it engages fields across the arts, humanities, legal studies, and social sciences. As an analytic, scholars engaging Diaspora are trying to get to the complexity of the concept through multiple disciplinary frameworks. For instance, Stephan Palmié, drawing on the work of Claude Lévi-Strauss, referring to a "descent" and "alliance" multidisciplinary debate about the development of the African Diaspora is a part of this process.[38]

In this perspective, the beginning of the category of descent could be traced to the Frazier-Herskovits debate.[39] The idea of common African origin has received support from scholars such as Roger Bastide, Melville Herskovits, and Gonzalo Aguirre Beltrán.[40] Their works have become part of the historical narrative of the African Diaspora. Herskovits is perhaps the best known of these scholars. In *The Myth of the Negro Past*, he argues that there were African survivals or retentions among peoples of African descent in the Americas and challenges the view that "Africanisms have disappeared as a result of the pressures exerted by the experience of slavery on all aboriginal modes of thought or behavior."[41]

Subsequently, other scholars, sometimes referred to as neo-Herskovitsians, have explored not so much African survivals and retentions but cultural transformations over time as a basis for black articulation. This approach highlights the significance of historical linkages among black peoples through the clustering of enslaved African migrants who impacted cultural development in the Western Hemisphere and throughout the globe. David Eltis, a major contributor to *Trans-Atlantic Slave Trade: A Database*, argues that enslaved individuals were "supplied from a small number of African embarkation points—most of them located on a two-hundred-mile range of the coast."[42] Gwendolyn Hall adds the assertion that "Africans were often clustered in the Americas rather than randomized or deliberately fragmented."[43] These views emphasize, as Michael A. Gomez affirms, that Africans forcefully brought to the Americas had certain coherent perspectives and beliefs about the universe and their place in it and they selected elements of various cultures from Africa (America and Europe as well), ranging from music, art, and folklore to language, to develop a new community.[44]

The neo/Herskovitsian proponents contest the argument by other scholars, such as E. Franklin Frazier, Sidney Mintz, and Richard Price, that black peoples in the New World were to a significant degree products of colonial or New World formation and African cultures were not transported to the Americas. In fact, according to Mintz and Price in *The Birth of the African American Culture*, "While immense quantities of knowledge, information, and belief must have been transported in the minds of the enslaved, they were not able to transfer the human complement of their traditional institution to the New World."[45] This view is often linked to the "creationist" or "creolization" school of thought.

Afro-Atlantic dialogue, as a metaphor, whether or not it fits into this view of "alliance" as argued by Palmié, can be seen as critical for black connections as well. This view adds to the literature on the significance of the coevalness of the African and African-descended peoples' interaction. It argues that "Africa is not to its Diaspora as the past is to the present."[46] At the same time, it challenges the previous reification of the past and neglect of Africa of the creationists and retentionists as well as cultural theorists (such as Paul Gilroy). As Kevin A. Yelvington contends, dialogue consists of

> multiparty interactions of material, ideational, and discursive phenomena, among others, in complex relationships characterized more often than not by an unequal distribution of power; not between fixed objects, but a process of mutual influence and conditioning that is itself already part of an ongoing dialogic process where "rhetorics of self-making" (pace Battaglia 1995) play a crucial role.[47]

As argued by J. Lorand Matory, the dialogue between Africans and their descendants is imbued with economic, political, literary, religious, and musical significance.[48] Furthermore, Matory summarizes this dialogue as follows:

> The metaphor of "dialogue" would instead highlight the ways in which the mutual gaze between Africans and African Americans, multidirectional travel and migration between the two hemispheres, the movement of publications, commerce, and so forth have shaped African and African American cultures in tandem, over time, and at the same time. It highlights the ways in which cultural artifacts, images and practices do not simply "survive" or endure through "memory"; they are, rather, interpreted and reproduced for diverse contemporary purposes by actors with culturally diverse repertoires, diverse interests, and diverse degrees of power to assert them. As in a literal dialogue, such interpretations and reproductions can also be silenced, articulated obliquely, paraphrased, exaggerated, or quoted mockingly as well.[49]

Indeed, rather than an Afro-Atlantic dialogue alone, it is a global African dialogue (as in the worldwide population of Africans and their descendants) that includes the Mediterranean Sea and the Indian Ocean.

Fundamentally, the African Diaspora is engaged with all of these approaches and more. As often portrayed, these approaches are not mutually exclusive, particularly in examining the workings of the African Diaspora. These schools of thought more or less emphasize narratives of black connections across time and place that are embedded in an idea of common African origin that actually comes out of the experience of, and resistance to, black abjection. In this view of the African Diaspora, the creationist approach emphasizes the significance of the impact of black abjection on the destruction of African communities in the New World. The neo/Herskovitsian perspective highlights the influence of ideas of origin and their importance to the formation of Afro-American societies, whereas the Afro-Atlantic dialogue engages collective consciousness as continuous and persistent interactions with African and African-descended interlocutors. Ultimately, what is being debated here is the nature, level, significance, and consequence of these connections, and even lack thereof.

Diasporic Phenomenology

In adding to this, phenomenologically, diasporic peoples, such as Maroons, are involved in multifaceted conversations with a range of entities. At varying degrees, Maroons engage all these schools of thought. In resisting black abjection, Maroons create new or modified traditions and customs in adapting to their new environments, as in the viewpoint of the creolist (or even neo-Herskovitsian). Turning to origin, they attempt to preserve ancestral traditional practices under a metaphoric understanding of African cultural retentions and survivals (the Herskovitsian view). In furthering solidarity consciousness, Maroons are partaking in dialogue with other black interlocutors through the media, transnational networks, visits, travel, and even migration (Afro-Atlantic dialogue perspective).

More so, Maroons—similar to other African-descended communities— are interacting with academics that often subscribe to one or more of these various schools of thought as they relate to the African Diaspora. In discussion with Maroons, many referenced and had academic books in their collection that they obtained from scholars whom many have maintained contact with. Furthermore, Maroons are involved in Afro-Atlantic dialogue not only with contemporary black people—including politicians, educators, and artists—but with the ancestors and unborn generations. In turn, Jamaican Maroons, consciously and subconsciously, like other diasporic peoples, draw from all these conversations that inform their engagement with the African Diaspora.

Conclusion

The Workings of Diaspora examines the lived experiences of the African Diaspora in Jamaican Maroon communities. In the re-conceptualization of the African Diaspora, it shows the significance of the notion as an analytical tool. The book reveals how particular black communities uniquely engage the core elements of the African Diaspora: abjection, origin, and collective consciousness. The way these elements are engaged tells us not only why the African Diaspora is used but specifically how the group distinctively uses it to improve black social, economic, and political standing. It highlights how these distinctive communities become a part of the African Diaspora. Also, the book draws attention to how phenomenologically Maroons in and of themselves engage academic (such as the neo-Herskovitsian, creationist, Afro-Atlantic dialogic views) and non-academic approaches in the workings of the African Diaspora. For Jamaican Maroon communities, the critical practice, articulation, and politics of the African Diaspora are engaged in a quest for sovereignty against the discourse of inhumanity to black peoples.

Notes

1. Ferron Williams, interview by author, Accompong Town, St. Elizabeth, Jamaica, January 7, 2012.

2. Parts of this chapter were previously published in *Symbolism* and used with permission. Mario Nisbett, "African Diasporic Traditional Symbols and Claims," in *Rüdiger Ahrens, Florian Kläger*, Keith A. Sandiford and Klaus Stierstorfer (eds.) of *Symbolism: An International Annual of Critical Aesthetics*, Volume 16, Berlin, Germany: De Gruyter, 2016, pp. 117–138. Mario Nisbett, "Defining and Utilizing Diaspora: Towards a Path to African Post-Development," *Contemporary Journal of African Studies* 8, Nos. 1 & 2 (2021).

3. "UNESCO giving US$900,000 to Moore Town Maroons," *Jamaica Observer* (Kingston), June 09, 2004, accessed December 04, 2020, https://www.jamaicaobserver.com/news/60961_UNESCO-giving-US-900-000-to-Moore-Town-Maroons.

4. Sabelo J. Ndlovu-Gatsheni, *Coloniality of Power in Postcolonial Africa: Myths of Decolonization* (Dakar: Codesria, 2013), 3.

5. Khachig Tölölyan, "Rethinking Diaspora(s): Stateless Power in the Transnational Moment," *Diaspora: A Journal of Transnational Studies* 5, no. 1 (1996): 8; Brent Hayes Edwards, "The Uses of Diaspora," *Social Text* 19, no. 1 (2001): 1; Darlene Clark Hines, Trica Danielle Keaton, and Stephen Small, eds., *Black Europe and the African Diaspora* (Urbana: University of Illinois Press, 2009).

6. Tölölyan, "Rethinking Diaspora(s)," 8.

7. Kim Butler, "Defining Diaspora, Refining a Discourse," *Diaspora* 10, no. 2 (2001): 193; James Clifford, "Diasporas," *Cultural Anthropology* 9, no. 3 (1994): 310; Rainer Baubo̊ck and Thomas Faist, *Diaspora and Transnationalism: Concepts, Theories and Methods* (Amsterdam: Amsterdam University Press, 2010), 14.

8. Evelyn Hu-DeHart, "The Future of "Diaspora" in Diaspora Studies: Has the Word Run Its Course?" *Verge: Studies in Global Asias* 1, no. 1 (2015): 42.

9. Earl Lewis, "To Turn as on a Pivot: Writing African Americans into a History of Overlapping Diasporas," *American Historical Review* 100, no. 3 (1995): 767.

10. George Shepperson, "African Diaspora: Concept and Context," in *Global Dimensions of the African Diaspora*, ed. Joseph Harris (Washington, DC: Howard University Press, 1982), 47.

11. William E. B. Du Bois and Brent Hayes Edwards, *The Souls of Black Folk* (Oxford: Oxford University Press, 2007), 2.

12. Joseph E. Harris, "Expanding the Scope of African Diaspora Studies: The Middle East and India, a Research Agenda," *Radical History Review* 87, no. 1 (2003): 158.

13. Colin A. Palmer, "Defining and Studying the Modern African Diaspora," *Journal of Negro History* 85, no. 1/2 (2000): 29.

14. Paul Tiyambe Zeleza, "The Challenges of Studying the African Diasporas," *African Sociological Review/Revue Africaine De Sociologie* 12, no. 2 (2008): 7.

15. Stuart Hall, "New Cultures for Old," in *A Place in the World? Places, Cultures and Globalization*, ed. John Allen and Doreen B. Massey (Oxford: Oxford University Press, 1995), 206.

16. Ibid.

17. Percy C. Hintzen and Jean Muteba Rahier, "Introduction," in *Global Circuits of Blackness: Interrogating the African Diaspora*, eds. Jean Muteba Rahier, Percy C. Hintzen, and Felipe Smith (Urbana: University of Illinois Press, 2010), x.

18. Sandra So Hee Chi Kim, "Redefining Diaspora Through a Phenomenology of Postmemory," *Diaspora: A Journal of Transnational Studies* 16, no. 3 (2007): 338–339.

19. Julia Kristeva, *Powers of Horror: An Essay of Abjection* (New York: Columbia University Press, 1984), 11.

20. Jennifer Daryl Slack, "The Theory and Method of Articulation in Cultural Studies," in *Stuart Hall: Critical Dialogues in Cultural Studies*, eds. David Morley and Kuan-Hsing Chen (New York: Taylor & Francis, 1996), 114.

21. Lawrence Grossberg, "On Postmodernism and Articulation: An Interview with Stuart Hall," in *Stuart Hall: Critical Dialogues in Cultural Studies*, eds. David Morley and Kuan-Hsing Chen (New York: Taylor & Francis, 1996), 141–142.

22. Brent Hayes Edwards, *The Practice of Diaspora: Literature, Translation, and the Rise of Black Internationalism* (Cambridge, MA: Harvard University Press, 2003), 13–15.

23. John Fiske, "Open the Hallway: Some Remarks on the Fertility of Stuart Hall's Contribution to Critical Theory," in *Stuart Hall: Critical Dialogues in Cultural Studies*, eds. David Morley and Kuan-Hsing Chen (New York: Taylor & Francis, 1996), 213.

24. Ibid., 214.

25. Slack, "Theory and Method," 112.

26. Ibid.

27. Stuart Hall, "Cultural Identity and Diaspora," in *Identity: Community, Culture, Difference*, ed. Jonathan Rutherford (London: Lawrence & Wishart, 1990), 225.

28. Ibid.

29. Ibid., 226.

30. Ibid., 225.

31. Brent Hayes Edwards, "The Uses of Diaspora," *Social Text* 19, no. 1 (2001): 60.

32. Aisha Khan, "Material and Immaterial Bodies: Diaspora Studies and the Problem of Culture, Identity, and Race," *Small Axe* 19, no. 3 (2015): 47.

33. Ibid.

34. Michael Omi and Howard Winant, *Racial Formation in the United States: From the 1960s to the 1990s* (New York: Routledge, 1994), 55.

35. Kim, "Redefining Diaspora Through a Phenomenology of Postmemory," 337.

36. Ibid.

37. Khan, "Material and Immaterial Bodies," 43.

38. Stephan Palmié, "Afterword: Descent and Alliance in Afro-Atlantic Anthropology," *Zeitschrift Für Ethnologie* 136, no. 2 (2011): 401–415.

39. Jemima Pierre, *The Predicament of Blackness: Postcolonial Ghana and the Politics of Race* (Chicago: The University of Chicago Press, 2013), 194–195.

40. Roger Bastide, *African Civilisations in the New World* (New York: Harper & Row, 1971); Melville J. Herskovits, *The Myth of the Negro Past* (Boston: Beacon Press, 1958).

41. Herskovits, *The Myth of the Negro Past*, 3.

42. David Eltis, *The Rise of African Slavery in the Americas* (Cambridge, UK: Cambridge University Press, 2000), 252.

43. Gwendolyn Midlo Hall, *Slavery and African Ethnicities in the Americas: Restoring the Links* (Chapel Hill: University of North Carolina Press), 50, 55.

44. Michael A. Gomez, *Exchanging Our Country Marks: The Transformation of African Identities in the Colonial and Antebellum South* (Chapel Hill: The University of North Carolina Press, 1998), 4.

45. Sidney W. Mintz and Richard Price, *The Birth of African-American Culture: An Anthropological Perspective* (Boston: Beacon Press, 1992), 18–19.

46. J. Lorand Matory, "From 'Survival' to 'Dialogue': Analytic Tropes in the Study of African-Diaspora Cultural History," in *Transatlantic Caribbean: Dialogues of People, Practices, Ideas*, eds. Ingrid Kummels, Claudia Rauhut, Stefan Rinke, and Birte Timm (London: Transcript-Verlag, 2014), 48.

47. Kevin A. Yelvington, "The Anthropology of Afro-Latin America and the Caribbean: Diasporic Dimensions Source," *Annual Review of Anthropology* 30 (2001): 240–241.

48. Matory, "From 'Survival' to 'Dialogue,'" 45.

49. Ibid., 47.

1

Jamaican Maroons

History, Politics, and Culture

> The Sankofa bird is significant of what the Maroons have been, are today, and our intention, too, as well. The eggs represent the future. Now the bird takes oil from the tail feather so that it can maintain the rest of the body to preserve the future. So, what we say is that we take things from a long time ago from our fore-parents' time and keep [them] today for the generation to come.
>
> —Marcia Douglas of Charles Town Maroon Community[1]

Introduction

THIS CHAPTER PRESENTS A SUMMARY of multiple perspectives on the meaning and history of the Jamaican Maroons (focusing on the Accompong community) of the African Diaspora, spanning more than three hundred and fifty years. Scholarly literature, archival accounts, oral histories, and other sources of data have to be considered in exploring this subject matter.[2] From Maroon and non-Maroon alike, the information is found not only in books, newspapers, and magazines but also on the Internet, including YouTube, Facebook, and Twitter.[3] Drawn from the multidisciplinary subfield of Maroon studies, some of the information is conflicting and contradictory.[4] In any case, this descriptive and chronologically arranged synopsis provides the background needed for the later discussion about the links among Maroons, the African Diaspora, and sovereignty.

The Meaning of "Maroons" and their Formations

Before exploring the history, it is important to present a clear definition of who the Maroons are. What it is to be Maroon has changed over the last five centuries in the Americas. As communities, Maroons have faced significant historical and political erasure. With a clearer definition, it is possible to understand Maroon communities' significance and their place in the African Diaspora.

The word "Maroon" comes from the Spanish word *cimarrón*. According to the scholars José Juan Arrom and Manuel Antonio García Arévalo, cimarrón, which had an Arawakan/Taino root, was originally used to refer to feral cattle, then to Amerindians, and finally to peoples of African descent who had fled from slavery on Hispaniola.[5] As the anthropologist Richard Price has argued, the word was then adopted as "Maroon" and "Seminole" in English, "Marron" in Dutch and French, and "Bosnegers" in Dutch Guiana (Suriname).[6]

To grasp the Maroon experience, scholars require a comprehensive understanding of the concept. At the most fundamental level, Maroons are considered to be formerly enslaved individuals and their descendants who established their own autonomous communities in various parts of the Americas (as well as Africa and Asia).[7] In the written literature, Maroons are also variously referred to as fugitive slaves, runaway slaves, and self-liberated formerly enslaved persons.

As we engage the concept, it is important to familiarize ourselves with Maroons' own response to how they are named. Maroons, at least in Jamaica, loosely refer to themselves as "Maroons" but also consider themselves in their language of Kromanti as "Fiiman" (Freeman).[8] According to Colonel (the title refers to the political head of the Jamaican Maroon communities) Wallace Sterling (1995–present) of Moore Town, political leader of the Jamaican Maroon communities:

> Let's put it this way: to begin with, the word "Maroon" was not used in a positive sense in describing our foreparents. It was more of a derogatory way of describing them. To that extent, our foreparents had never generally called themselves Maroon but would have referred to themselves as *Yenkunkun*. "Yenkunkun" here means a people who are self-reliant, a people who are independent, people who live and work together for the good of everyone. So, it was some sort of brotherhood, some sort of communal thing. So even today, we as descendants of Maroons refer to ourselves at Yenkunkun *Pikibo*. That means we are the descendants of those who were here before us, and those of our foreparents who chose to live together to fight for their own common good, to oppose the slavery they were living under.[9]

Also, the former Colonel Noel Prehay (c. 1983–2016) of Scot's Hall Maroon community, in a speech on August 1, 2012 on the Emancipation Day holiday in the English-speaking Caribbean, stated that Yenkunkun Pikibo, which is a Kromanti term, means "free and independent people."[10] In June 2011 at Charles Town Maroon community's Quao Day celebration, former Colonel Prehay (c. 1983–2016) added there was no such thing as "Maroon," and it makes him unhappy to hear people speak of Maroons.[11]

On the other hand, many Maroons accept the name of Maroon but challenge the Western interpretation of the word.[12] The Accompong Town tour guide Lawrence Rowe defines the word "Maroon" as freedom fighter, although he, like many other Maroons, is aware that to the Spanish and the British the word meant "wild and untamed savage."[13] According to Melville Currie of Accompong Town, a local historian and Deputy Colonel:

> If you look for the word "Maroon" in the dictionary, you will find "wild, untamed or to be cut off." We *were* wild. The British called us the wild and the untamed ones because they could not tame us to bow to them. We were living in the woods and all that. When the Treaty was signed, we were cut off from the rest of Jamaica, so we were Marooned. We are the Marooned ones. We were Marooned by the parishes of St. James, Westmoreland, Trelawny, and St. Elizabeth. We were Marooned from the rest of the island.[14]

In other words, from this perspective, Maroons are free men, women, and children with the vision to separate themselves from colonial and oppressive regimes to create independent communities. Indeed, freedom and self-reliance, as opposed to a wild cow, defines their core meaning.

The relationship between the concepts of Maroons and marronage is also important to understand. Marronage is the process of becoming or the state of being Maroon. Marronage could occur through the act of an individual, in the way that Frederick Douglass and Esteban Montejo of Cuba illustrate, or of a group.[15] The main destinations of these individuals or groups were to uninhabited areas (such as the woods), urban areas (sometimes referred to as urban marronage), and overseas, which historian Neville Hall refers to as "maritime marronage."[16] The destination of the unoccupied area was popular in both the islands and mainland Americas. Rural-to-urban (and sometimes urban-to-urban) flight was common not only in the small Caribbean islands but also in Brazil, Cuba, Mexico, Peru, Saint-Domingue, and the United States.[17]

There are two broad forms of marronage—petit and grand. Petit marronage was the temporary flight from a plantation or colonial authority for a limited time period. This was prevalent in both the small islands and the mainland Americas and appears to have been particularly high on small islands when the vegetation had mostly been cleared. The literature points to the varied response of the slaveholders, ranging from no punishment to whipping or even outright murder.

Grand marronage, which was seen as the greater threat to slaveholders, was often an intended permanent flight of individuals from a plantation or some other colonial authority. This form of marronage occurred throughout the Americas, whether on small islands or in mainland regions. Grand marronage was possible in the small islands during the early colonial period for some time but was curtailed after most of the lands had been occupied by plantations. Here, this form of marronage often involved maritime marronage, which saw some individuals fleeing from one Caribbean island to another and others sailing as far away as mainland North America.[18]

A number of definitions have been presented for the final destination of the individuals involved in grand marronage: Maroon communities. Communities of Maroons are variously referred to as *mocambo* and *quilombo* in Brazil and *palenque*, *cumbe*, and *ranchería* in Spanish colonies.[19] These words are often used interchangeably, but there are subtle differences in their use. According to Gabino La Rosa Corzo, a palenque is a socioeconomic unit in which a group of runaway slaves tries to live together.[20] A cumbe is also referred to generally as a settlement of runaway slaves. In contrast, a ranchería is considered a temporary settlement of runaway slaves, often having a group of small houses that provided temporary shelter.[21] This definition presents the problem of how long is temporary, and who is doing the defining. Stuart B. Schwartz informs us that the term mocambo originated from a West Central African Mbundu word for hideout. According to him, quilombo, too, is derived from Mbundu, but it referred to an encampment of any group of outlaws before being primarily employed to describe mainly fugitive slave communities.[22] For the historians João José Reis and Flávio dos Santos Gomes, based on Portuguese and Brazilian law, groups that are referred to as quilombos could be as small as four or five runaway slaves and could even include non-slave members.[23]

There is a need to re-examine the concepts of cumbe, Maroon community, mocambo, quilombo, and ranchería. Some scholars, particularly Reis and Gomes, believe that recent studies of quilombos have pointed to the difficulty of trying to establish a single model for the phenomenon other than defining the community simply as a group of settled fugitive slaves.[24] Yet the idea of "settled fugitive slaves" is itself problematic. The common factor in these groups is that they are independent communities that were oftentimes in an adversarial relationship with colonial societies, including the societies they may have fled from, which were usually but not exclusively comprised of formerly enslaved individuals.

Arguably, communities of Maroons were and are autonomous zones where liberated men and women from slaveholding regimes or other hegemonic powers implemented their vision of a self-governing community. Maroon communities, in a climate of appalling violence and sharing a common experience of abjection, presented a radical break from some of the most exploitative regimes in the early modern Americas. These communities today are the legacies of not only resistance to slavery but collaborations among diverse peoples—mainly those of African descent—in resisting slavery, colonialism, and the Western hegemonic order. These communities led to the emergence of several distinctively unique peoples and cultures throughout the Caribbean (Jamaican Maroons), Central America (Miskito-Zambo), North America (Black Seminoles), and South America (Saramaka).

Maroons and the Colonial Era

Now let us turn specifically to the emergence of the Maroon communities in Jamaica. Most of the information—especially in the academic literature—about the Jamaican Maroon communities covers the colonial period of Jamaica, which lasted about three hundred years. The present summary, chronologically arranged, will focus on the emergence and formation of the culture and identity of the Jamaican Maroons as well as the history of their political struggle of resistance.

The history of the Maroons begins in colonial Spanish Jamaica. The Spanish invaders first settled in Jamaica in 1509. Soon afterwards, in 1517, the first enslaved Africans were brought to Jamaica by the Spanish colonizers. They were transported to the island to replace indigenous Tainos, who had been forced to work in the colonizers' fields and mines, resulting in their numbers being decimated by warfare, disease, and suicide. A number of these enslaved Africans resisted enslavement and formed some of the earliest Maroon communities in the interior of Jamaica during the Spanish colonial period.[25]

In 1655, the English invaded Spanish Jamaica, causing an increase in the population of Maroons. At this time, many enslaved Africans seized the opportunity to establish communities in the mountains of Jamaica. Subsequently, the largely English and Scottish population began sugar cultivation, which demanded a significant increase in labor, increasing the number of enslaved Africans. They were brought primarily from West and West Central Africa, with a few from East Africa. Many of the newly enslaved Africans ran away to join or form their own camps and communities in the hills and mountains. At times, these different groups of Maroons would harass the English and raid the plantations. In the latter half of the seventeenth century into the early eighteenth, there was a low intensity but continuous war between the various Maroon groups and the British, collectively referred to as the First Maroon War. In the 1730s, the British intensified their war efforts against the various groups of Maroons. In strategic response to the warfare, the many different Maroon bands coalesced into two major groups: The Windward and Leeward Maroons.

The Windward Maroons, established primarily in the eastern mountains of Jamaica, had semi-permanent and permanent settlements called Nanny Town, New Nanny Town, Molly Town, and Crawford Town.[26] Their nucleus is believed to have been the group referred to as the "Spanish Maroons" who had established a community before the full British takeover of Jamaica from the Spanish colonizers. They were loosely organized in relatively autonomous towns, Nanny and Quao being two of their most influential leaders.[27] The community's population is estimated to have been about 500 people around 1739 when they agreed to a treaty with the British.[28]

The groups that formed the Leeward Maroons came from a number of settlements in the west central interior of Jamaica, including the established communities of Cudjoe Town (later called Trelawny Town) and Accompong Town. The choice for the location of this cluster stemmed from the protection afforded by its location around a limestone formation called the Cockpit Country, which is characterized by sinkholes, steep hills, jagged rocks, and dense vegetation.[29] Although the Leeward Maroons trace their origin back to the period of Spanish colonization, most scholars argue that the groups came from the seventeenth- and early eighteenth-century slave rebellions during the period of British rule. It is argued that many of their members were born in Africa, and most were considered to be Akan.[30] Some of the leaders of this group, such as Cudjoe (Kojo) and Accompong, have come to occupy a central place in Jamaican historical narratives. The Leeward Maroons established a highly centralized form of political organization, with a population that around 1739 numbered about 500, just like the Windward Maroons.[31]

After many decades, the British government and the Maroons began to seek ways to bring the warfare to an end. Although both sides had suffered great losses, the British, having suffered considerably more defeats and fearing further unrest in the island, initiated peace talks. In the end, the British and the two Maroon groups made two separate treaties around 1739 (see Appendices I and II for copies of the Treaties). The ability of groups of the formerly enslaved to force the British into an agreement to recognize their autonomy or sovereignty is considered a milestone in African Diaspora history.

These Treaties are highly significant for understanding the Jamaican Maroon communities, particularly concerning matters of sovereignty. It will be demonstrated later that the Treaties are one of the bases of claims to sovereignty over territory as a separate nation. In addition, they are the basis for post-colonial relations between the state and the Maroons. In later chapters, these critical issues will be discussed further.

Over the course of the eighteenth century, there were significant changes in the Maroon communities that resulted in their reconfiguration. This applied particularly to claims to territory (drastically impacted by the Treaties).[32] For both the Leeward and Windward Maroon groups, there were unclear and conflicting interpretations about the location and size of their territories. Initially, the Leeward Maroons, who lived in Trelawny Town (Cudjoe Town) in St. James Parish and Accompong Town in St. Elizabeth, made territorial claims to a sizeable portion of western Jamaica. [33] The territorial claims of the Windward Maroons were to their settlements in Crawford Town in St. George Parish and New Nanny Town in Portland Parish. Over time, different claims to territory were made by both groups as their members began to develop new settlements elsewhere.[34]

Subsequently, the two different Maroon groups started to expand and build new settlements. Around 1749, a group from Crawford Town left and established Scot's Hall in St. Mary Parish, acknowledged by the colonial authorities two years later.[35] In 1754, after an internal conflict led to the destruction of Crawford Town, it was deserted, and its members formed Charles Town several miles away in Portland Parish. Also, in the mid-1750s, a group of Maroons in Trelawny Town separated into a different settlement called Furry's Town.[36] The colonial authorities ordered the group to move back into the boundary of Trelawny Town, but instead it set up a new town close to Trelawny Town without integrating into the older settlement. In the early 1760s, Clash, a leader from New Nanny Town, attempted to establish a splinter group of Maroons in Bath, but the colonial authorities never recognized the settlement.[37] Nevertheless, the British authorities were somewhat flexible in their recognition of the emerging communities and their claims to territory.

From the literature, it seems that the relevance of these developments relates to the final ability of the British colonial authority to define the territorial boundaries of the Maroon communities with the use of force. However, British action to enforce their authority did not come without resistance and challenge as the Maroons asserted their autonomy and sovereignty.

Before the end of the eighteenth century, one of the Maroon communities (Cudjoe Town/Trelawny Town) was destroyed by the British in what is referred to as the Second Maroon War.[38] Essentially, in 1795, the Maroons of Trelawny Town (along with Furry's Town) chose to fight the colonial authorities because they believed the British were infringing on what was in effect their autonomy and sovereignty.[39] It is not entirely clear why the Accompong Maroons disagreed with the Trelawny Town Maroons about going to war, but the group reportedly sided with the British. On the other hand, the Windward Maroons, whom their Treaty stipulated were to help suppress any rebellion, did not get involved. The Governor, Alexander Lindsay, expected a few minor skirmishes at Trelawny Town (Cudjoe Town), but ended up in a war that lasted months.[40] After the war, the victorious British deported the Trelawny Town Maroons to Nova Scotia and later Sierra Leone.[41] Based on the literature, this also suggests that the British had the ability to assert their authority through force to place limitations on Maroon sovereignty and autonomy. This ability is evident, in this case, in the article of the Treaty stipulating the imperative of suppression of rebellion, which was adhered to by some groups and rejected by others.

The contemporary organization, including the political and social configuration of the Maroon communities, began to take shape. At the turn of the nineteenth century, according to Maroon oral histories, in defiance of the terms of the written Treaties, the Maroons selected their leaders, who were called chief or "colonel." However, scholars have highlighted British archival documentation challenging this interpretation, with British officials at times selecting some of the colonels. Internally, the communities' political organization was formulated around a cabinet of captains and majors which served as a council or committee to govern the community.[42] For the most part, each colonel and his council had executive, legislative, and judicial rights over their communities. Each of the communities operated autonomously and dealt with the British separately.

Over time the Maroons came to be organized into four distinct and recognized communities: Accompong Town, Charles Town, Moore Town (formerly called New Nanny Town), and Scot's Hall.[43] Later, Moore Town would expand to encompass a number of affiliated districts that included Cornwall Barracks, Cornwall Pen, Nottingham Pen, Ginger House, Comfort Castle, Hayfield, Seaman's Valley, Brownsfield, and Kent.[44] The colonial authorities' recognition of the size of the Maroon territorial lands ranged from as low as about 200 acres to over 2,500 acres.[45] The Maroons in the west (Leeward Maroons) actually lost one of their two communities, and the land of the community that survived was never increased formally by the colonial state. However, the Maroons in the east were able to build new communities and expand their territories in a way that was acknowledged by the colonial state. The three original communities there had varying degrees of state intervention in their internal affairs. The colonial state claimed all of Jamaica, but the Maroons were able to gain territory from colonial Jamaica.

The British authorities did adhere to and accept some Maroons' claims to a degree of autonomy. In most of the settlements, the Maroons were able to increase their acknowledged holdings over the decades. However, this entailed Maroons challenging the colonial state over land in just about every decade from the 1740s to the 1960s (the end of the colonial period).[46] Overall, claims to territory were a negotiated process involving the British use of force, resistance and rejection by the Maroons, and accommodation by both sides, including British acquiescence to Maroon claims.

Over the centuries, the main economic activity of the communities has been farming.[47] Maroons have grown a variety of agricultural goods, such as coffee, pimento, arrowroot, ginger, and tobacco.[48] The Maroons also engaged in selling livestock, such as hogs and chickens, and manufactured goods.[49] The Maroons also earned income by providing services to the colonial government and the settlers.[50] In the eighteenth and nineteenth centuries, Maroons participated in military service to the colonial state, including hunting runaway enslaved individuals and assisting in suppressing insurrections.[51] The Maroons also provided service to the colonial government in cutting and repairing roads.[52]

In the eighteenth and nineteenth centuries, Maroons had a continual struggle over sovereignty. Claims of the disorderliness of Maroons served as a technology of control and to legitimize interventions in their communities. British authorities passed a number of laws (unilaterally) to constrain Maroons' political leadership, economic activities, mobility, relations with the enslaved, and internal judicial systems. In many instances, the Maroons ignored or challenged these infringements on their autonomy.

In the immediate post-emancipation period, the British increasingly attempted to curtail Maroon autonomy. With the ending of slavery in 1834, the colonial authorities felt that they no longer needed Maroons as a tracking force and sought to assimilate the group into the wider Jamaican population. In 1842, legislation was passed to abrogate the Treaties through the Maroon Lands Allotment Act. The law sought to divide up the communally owned Maroon lands into individual parcels for their members. But the Maroons, particularly in Accompong Town, rejected and ignored what they saw as an unlawful unilateral act of the colonial government.[53] The British authorities did not force the issue of immediate Maroon assimilation. Nevertheless, they relied on the Maroons as a military force for a few post-emancipation rebellions. Most noteworthy, some of the Maroons supported the colonial authorities' suppression of the Morant Bay Rebellion of 1865 led by Paul Bogle.[54]

From the turn of the twentieth century until Jamaican independence (1962), the Maroon communities faced increasing challenges in their efforts to maintain their autonomy and sovereignty over their territory, which they sought to preserve and expand in both de jure and de facto terms. The colonial government sought to change the terms of the Treaties by converting the sovereign status of the Maroons to "special status," even while continuing to acknowledge some limited form of Maroon political authority by receiving its delegations and participating in ceremonial activities. The result of the British efforts was a steady weakening of Maroon political institutions and judicial autonomy. For instance, many judicial court cases began to be tried outside of the Maroon communities.[55]

The written and oral literature indicates that Maroons were in a constant struggle to enforce or maintain their sovereignty against the colonial state: a "war of position" with the colonial state that resulted in considerable de facto shifts in autonomy and sovereignty. Over the 224 years of the British treaty agreements and colonial rule of Jamaica, at times, the Maroons were subjected to and integrally absorbed into the colonial state, while at other times, they were de facto independent communities.

Maroons and the Post-Colonial Era

In post-colonial Jamaica, there are still four Maroon communities. The Maroons' relationship with the post-colonial state is cooperative at times, and at other times tense. In particular, the relationship is contested and fraught concerning Maroon sovereignty. In many ways, the ambiguity, tenuousness, and ambivalence that characterized the Maroons' relationship with the colonial state have continued with the post-colonial state.

For the sake of brevity, I will focus on the basic cultural contours of the population of Maroons (particularly Accompong), highlighting the culturally distinct aspects of the people, but noting overlaps not just divergence. Often, the difference from the wider Jamaican culture is attributed in the literature to a greater autonomy and degree of "African-ness" in the Maroons' cultural practices and expressions.

It is highly debated whether Jamaican Maroons are culturally the same as the rest of Jamaica or a distinctive group.[56] For instance, the historian Mavis Campbell considers the Maroons to be culturally no different from other Jamaicans. On the other hand, the anthropologist Kenneth Bilby contends that the Maroons are ethnic groups that differ culturally despite significant areas of overlap with the rest of Jamaica.[57] He effectively argues this point because Maroons possess their own "religious beliefs, pharmacopeia, oral traditions, music, dance, languages, and other distinctive forms of expressive culture."[58] More in line with Bilby's view, I support the stance that Maroons are a distinct variant of the overall Jamaican culture.

To further explain the culture of the Maroons, it is important to gain a sense of their numbers. The Maroon population is comprised of many thousands of people, mainly of African descent, living in the four specific settlements and beyond. The total number of Jamaican Maroons is hard to estimate. In the 1980s, according to former Accompong Maroon Colonel Meredith Rowe (1993–1998), there were about 100,000 Maroons living in Jamaica.[59] In the mid-1990s, the Maroon leader and author Bev Carey estimated that there were about 500,000 Jamaican Maroons worldwide (outside of Jamaica, mostly in the UK and US, as well as Canada and other Caribbean islands).[60]

In particular, estimates of the population of the Accompong Town settlement, considered the largest and most vocal on the matter of sovereignty, have some discrepancies. In 2012, the community members and leaders presented figures ranging from 800 to 1,800 people living in the settlement.[61] In 2009, according to a survey conducted by the Government of Jamaica through the Social Development Commission (SDC), the community's population was 808 persons in 209 households.[62] At that time, the population had slightly more females than males.[63] The percentage of people under the age of 30 was about 45 percent of the population (more youthful than the Jamaican national average), but at the same time those 60 years and over were about 21 percent of the population (9 percent higher than the Jamaican national average).[64] Accompong Town is therefore over-represented in both younger and older people compared with the overall Jamaican population.

To the community of Accompong Maroons, and similarly, the other three Maroon communities, networks and claims of belonging extend beyond the physical community. Outside Accompong Town are thousands of Accompong Maroons living in neighboring communities such as Aberdeen, Santa Cruz, and Montego Bay, while others are as far away as Kingston, New York, and London.[65] Community leaders and members estimate that there are a total of 12,000–30,000 Accompong Maroons worldwide.[66] It is not uncommon to see many individuals moving between Accompong Town and other communities in Jamaica.

The origin of the Maroons is important for identity formation, as a signifier of cultural differences that are also concrete inherited practices. On the whole, the literature indicates that the Maroons share the same general origin as the overall larger black Jamaican population. The predominant issues covered in the literature are about the African influence and creolization of the Maroon communities. Overall, African origin is listed in general and at times focused on specific cultural groups, such as Akan, Igbos, Kongoleses, and Yorubas, which are argued to have had the greatest influence.[67]

The Maroons in Jamaica make specific claims to an Akan origin, as will be shown in later chapters. What makes Maroons different are their extant cultural practices, their material conditions, and their political organization, which may indeed be explained in terms of specific African origin.

In the religious realm, Maroons are similar to other black Jamaicans in practicing a variety of belief systems. The Accompong Maroons' main official religious belief system is Christianity. There are currently seven churches, among them the Church of Jamaica and Grand Cayman, Church of God

International, Assembly of Zion, Seventh Day Baptist Church, and New Testament Church of God.[68] But, there are also practitioners of Kromanti Play, Obeah, Myalism, and Rastafari(anism). Some of these alternatives to Christianity will be explored further in chapter four.[69]

Overall, the Maroons are not completely monolithic. Culturally, Maroons may both converge with and diverge from the wider Jamaican population. However, they have more in common with the greater Jamaican society than difference.

Conclusion

There are various views on the meaning and historical, political, and cultural development of the Maroon communities of Jamaica. This chapter has described the over three hundred years' history of resistance and struggle centered on the issues of freedom and sovereignty. The significance of being Maroon and a resistor to slavery and colonialism is highly contested by the Maroons themselves and researchers into their history. Certainly, the history of their struggle is an uneven one. In many respects, the Maroons have been in a "war of position" with the colonial and post-colonial states of Jamaica. Jamaican Maroons may have more similarities with the wider Jamaican community, but there are some differences. In the following chapters, the dynamics of Maroon communities, the African Diaspora, and sovereignty will all be explored in detail.

Notes

1. Marcia Douglas, interview by the author, Charles Town, Portland, Jamaica, January 06, 2012; Mario Nisbett, "African Diasporic Traditional Symbols and Claims," *Symbolism: An International Annual of Critical Aesthetics* 16 (2016): 117.

2. Only a few comprehensive works examine the history and overall development of Maroon communities in Jamaica and throughout the world. In 1973, Richard Price edited the seminal work *Maroon Societies*, which shows that marronage was much more frequent and widespread than previously assumed and elaborates on the characteristics of the Maroon communities. In 1984, a most significant work on the general British Caribbean, *Testing the Chains: Resistance to Slavery in the British West Indies*, by Michael Craton, focuses on various forms of resistance, especially marronage, mainly in Jamaica, Barbados, Antigua, Grenada, St. Vincent, and Dominica. In 1986, *Out of the House of Bondage*, edited by Gad Heuman, presents chapters that examine runaway enslaved individuals and Maroon communities in Africa (specifically Angola) and Barbados, Colonial North America, Jamaica, Saint Domingue, and

Suriname. In 1994, *Maroon Heritage: Archaeological, Ethnographic, and Historical Perspectives*, edited by E. Kofi Agorsah with Jamaican Maroon contributors, examines cultural innovation among Maroons, mainly in Jamaica, Mexico, and Suriname. Finally, in 2006, Alvin Thompson, in *Flight to Freedom*, tries to reassess the views and the interpretations of runaways' attempts to gain freedom and their efforts to maintain such freedoms throughout the Americas.

3. "Accompong Maroon Festival 2020," The Public Broadcasting Corporation of Jamaica, accessed November 23, 2020, https://www.youtube.com/watch?v=XwJfLqz67Xs; Accompong News (@AccompongNews), Twitter, December 30, 2020, https://twitter.com/AccompongNews.

4. In the last few decades, a few works have been published by Maroons about their own history and culture, including Milton C. McFarlane's *Cudjoe of Jamaica: Pioneer for Black Freedom in the New World* (1977); C. L. G. Harris and Charles Aarons' *On My Honour* (1988); Bev Carey's *The Maroon Story: The Authentic and Original History of the Maroons in the History of Jamaica, 1490–1880* (1997); C. L. G. Harris's *Teacha* (2004); and Norma Rowe-Edwards' *My Father Said* (2011). In addition, two Maroon descendants produced films on Maroon history and culture: Ashley McFarlane's *Re-Membering* (2011) and Roy Anderson's *Akwantu: The Journey* (2012) and *Queen Nanny: Legendary Maroon Chieftainess* (2016). There are many website pages about Maroons, but Maroons run only two: the websites of Accompong Town at https://www.accompong-gov.org/ and Charles Town at http://www.Maroons-jamaica.com/q/.

5. Richard Price, "Maroons in Anthropology," in *International Encyclopedia of the Social and Behavioral Sciences*, eds. Neil J. Smelser and Paul B. Baltes (Oxford: Elsevier Science, 2001), 9253; José Juan Arrom and Manuel Antonio García Arévalo, *Cimarrón* (Santo Domingo, Dominican Republic: [s.n.] 1986), 1.

6. Richard Price, ed., *Maroon Societies: Rebel Slave Communities in the Americas* (Baltimore: Johns Hopkins University Press, 1996), xii.

7. Alvin O. Thompson, *Flight to Freedom: African Runaways and Maroons in the Americas* (Kingston, Jamaica: University of West Indies Press, 2004), 124; Terry Weik, "The Archaeology of Maroon Societies in the Americas: Resistance, Cultural Continuity, and Transformation in the African Diaspora," *Historical Archaeology* 31, no. 2 (1997): 82.

8. Frank Lumsden, interview by author, Charles Town, Portland, Jamaica, December 06, 2011.

9. Wallace Sterling, interview by author, Moore Town, Portland, Jamaica, December 1, 2011.

10. Noel Prehay, "Introductory Remarks," (speech, Quao Day celebration, Scot's Hall, Jamaica, August 1, 2012).

11. Noel Prehay, "Welcome Remarks," (speech, Quao Day celebration, Charles Town, Jamaica, June 23, 2011).

12. "The Jamaican Maroons," CaribNation TV, accessed November 23, 2020, https://www.youtube.com/watch?v=-US3_OxhEsk; Queen Nanny of the Maroons, Facebook, accessed December 29, 2020, https://www.facebook.com/Queen.Nanny/;

Charles Town Maroons (@ctmaroons), Twitter, accessed December 30, 2020, https://twitter.com/ctmaroons.

13. Lawrence Rowe and Lance Ricketts, interview by author, Accompong Town, St. Elizabeth, Jamaica, January 8, 2012.

14. Melville Currie, interview by author, Accompong Town, St. Elizabeth, Jamaica, August 14, 2012.

15. Frederick Douglass fled from Maryland into the Northern States where slavery was not practiced. Esteban Montejo lived in the woods of Cuba for many years in isolation. Frederick Douglass, *Narrative of the Life of Frederick Douglass, an American Slave; My Bondage and My Freedom; Life and Times of Frederick Douglass* (New York: Literary Classics of the United States, 1994); Esteban Montejo and Miguel Barnet, *The Autobiography of a Runaway Slave* (New York: Meridian Books, 1969).

16. Neville A. T. Hall and B. W. Higman, *Slave Society in the Danish West Indies: St. Thomas, St. John, and St. Croix* (Baltimore: Johns Hopkins University Press, 1992), 124.

17. Thompson, *Flight to Freedom*, 104.

18. Hall and Higman, *Slave Society in the Danish West Indies*, 124–138; Polly Pope, "A Maroon Settlement on St. Croix," *Negro History Bulletin* 35, no. 7 (1972): 153–154; Waldemar Westergaard, *The Danish West Indies under Company Rule (1671–1754)* (New York: The Macmillan Company, 1917), 161. See Hilary Beckles, "From Land to Sea: Runway Barbados Slaves and Servants, 1630–1700," in *Out of the House of Bondage: Runaways, Resistance and Maroonage in Africa and the New World*, ed. Gad J. Heuman (London: Cass, 1986), 79.

19. Thompson, *Flight to Freedom*, 7; Price, "Maroons in Anthropology," 9253.

20. Gabino La Rosa Corzo, *Runaway Slave Settlements in Cuba: Resistance and Repression* (Chapel Hill: University of North Carolina Press, 2003), 8.

21. Ibid., 7.

22. Stuart B. Schwartz, *Slaves, Peasants, and Rebels: Reconsidering Brazilian Slavery* (Urbana: University of Illinois Press, 1992), 121, 125; Jan Vansina, "Quilombos on São Thomé, or In Search of Original Sources," *History in Africa* 23 (1996): 453–459.

23. Schwartz, *Slaves, Peasants, and Rebels*, 125.

24. Joao Jose Reis and Flavio dos Santos Gomes, "Quilombo: Brazilian Maroons during Slavery," *Cultural Survival Quarterly* 25, Issue 4 (2002): 19–20.

25. Kathleen Wilson, "The Performance of Freedom: Maroons and the Colonial Order in Eighteenth-Century Jamaica and the Atlantic Sound," *The William and Mary Quarterly* 66, no. 1 (2009): 69; Barbara Kopytoff, "The Development of Jamaican Ethnicity," *Caribbean Quarterly* 22, no. 2/3 (1976): 37.

26. Barbara Klamon Kopytoff, "The Maroons of Jamaica: An Ethnohistorical Study of Incomplete Polities, 1655–1905" (PhD diss., University of Pennsylvania, 1973), 37.

27. The following works explore the significance of Nanny of the Maroons: Alan Tuelon's "Nanny—Maroon Chieftainess," C. L. G. Harris's *The Chieftainess*, Marguerite Curtain's *Nanny, Queen of the Maroons*, Karla Gottlieb's *The Mother of Us All*, and Karl Phillpotts and Marjorie Gammon's *Nanny*.

28. Barbara K. Kopytoff, "The Early Political Development of Jamaican Maroon Societies," *The William and Mary Quarterly* 35, no. 2 (1978): 290, 298, 301.

29. Ibid., 290.
30. Ibid., 289, 292, 293.
31. Ibid., 301.
32. In the latter half of the eighteenth century and the early nineteenth, a few scholars, albeit in one-sided accounts, wrote about the early Maroon experience, providing more details of their early history. In 1774, Edward Long's *The History of Jamaica* was the first major publication that briefly addressed the Maroons' origin and early development. Long states that many enslaved Africans in different groups fled to the mountains of Jamaica after the transition from Spanish to British rule. They fought against the British in the following decades while groups of runaways were augmenting their population. He wrote about the signing of the Treaties and its implication for the early history of Jamaica. In 1801, Bryan Edwards and William Young's *An Historical Survey of the Island of Saint Domingo Together with an Account of the Maroon Negroes in the Island of Jamaica, and a History of the War in the West Indies, in 1793, and 1794*, presents the history of a few Caribbean islands including Jamaica. This manuscript, essentially a compilation of Edwards' earlier works by Young, provides information on the Maroons' origin, early development, and the Second Maroon War and its aftermath. In 1803, Robert Dallas's *The History of the Maroons, from Their Origin to the Establishment of Their Chief Tribe at Sierra Leone*, which followed along the lines of Long and Edwards/Young, was the first major publication to focus on the Jamaican Maroons. Dallas presents the Maroons' origin during the Spanish conquests and the Maroon numbers' eventual increase from the local plantations during various rebellions. He also examines the Treaties and the Second Maroon War. These manuscripts, including Robert Renny's *An History of Jamaica: with Observations on the Climate, Scenery, Trade, Productions, Negroes, Slave Trade, Diseases of Europeans, Customs, Manners, and dispositions of the Inhabitants; to Which is Added, an Illustration of the Advantages, Which are Likely to Result from the Abolition of the Slave Trade*, all provide a firsthand account of Maroon history in the seventeenth and eighteenth centuries.
33. Harris Cawley, interview by author, Accompong Town, St. Elizabeth, Jamaica, August 01, 2012; Hansley Reid, interview by author, Accompong Town, St. Elizabeth, Jamaica, December 21, 2011; James Chambers, interview by the author, Accompong Town, St. Elizabeth, Jamaica, December 22, 2011; Mann O. Rowe, interview by an unknown interviewer, undated, interview T265, African Caribbean Institute of Jamaica, Kingston, Jamaica.
34. Beverley Hall-Alleyne, "Asante Kotoko: The Maroons of Jamaica," *Newsletter: African-Caribbean Institute of Jamaica* no. 7 (1982): 13.
35. Barbara Klamon Kopytoff, "Jamaican Maroon Political Organization: The Effects of the Treaties," *Social and Economic Studies* 25, no. 2 (1976): 92.
36. Ibid.
37. Ibid., 93.
38. A handful of works examine the Second Maroon War in greater detail: Douglas Brymner's *The Jamaica Maroons: How They Came to Nova Scotia, How They Left It* (1894); Mavis Campbell's *Nova Scotia and the Fighting Maroons: A Documentary History* (1990); Lennox O'Riley Picart's *The Trelawny Maroons and Sir John Wen-*

tworth: The Struggle to Maintain their Culture, 1796–1800 (1993); Mavis Campbell and George Ross's *Back to Africa: George Ross and the Maroons: From Nova Scotia to Sierra Leone* (1993); Allister Hinds' *Deportees in Nova Scotia: The Jamaican Maroons 1796–1800* (1997); J. D. Lockett's "The Deportation of the Maroons of Trelawny Town to Nova Scotia, Then Back to Africa" (1999); and J. A. Fortin, "'Blackened Beyond Our Native Hue': Removal, Identity and the Trelawney Maroons on the Margins of the Atlantic World, 1796–1801" (2006).

39. Kenneth M. Bilby, *True-Born Maroons* (Gainesville: University Press of Florida, 2005), 378.

40. Ibid., 379.

41. Bilby, *True-Born Maroons*, 380–381; Wilson, "The Performance of Freedom," 72.

42. Kopytoff, "Maroons of Jamaica," 126; Hall-Alleyne, "Asante Kotoko," 13.

43. The first major lengthy piece by a historian on Maroon history is Mavis Campbell's *The Maroons of Jamaica, 1655–1796: A History of Resistance, Collaboration & Betrayal.* Campbell presents great detail on the history of the Maroons, focusing on the period 1655 to 1796. The book explores what Campbell considers to be the complicated connections among resistance, collaboration, and betrayal. She explores Maroons' resistance to slavery in the period between 1655 and 1738. She then examines Maroons' involvement in hunting runaways and suppressing slave uprisings in the post-treaty era. She also briefly engages Maroons' post-emancipation involvement in the suppression of rebellions. Campbell uses a wide range of sources but relies heavily on British sources, especially the *Journals of the Assembly of Jamaica* and Colonial Office records. One of her central and controversial arguments is that the Maroons were not reformists or revolutionaries but only fought for their own freedom.

44. Hall-Alleyne, "Asante Kotoko," 13.

45. Kopytoff, "The Maroons of Jamaica," 137, 142, 144, 335.

46. "Governor Offers the Maroons of Accompong Grant of More Lands," *Jamaica Standard* (Kingston), June 19, 1939; Daniel Lee Schafer, "The Maroons of Jamaica: African Slave Rebels in the Caribbean" (PhD diss., University of Minnesota, 1974), 174; Bev Carey, *The Maroon Story: The Authentic and Original History of the Maroons in the History of Jamaica, 1490–1880* (Gordon Town, Jamaica: Agouti Press, 1997), 559; Hilary F. Smith, "Stakeholder Involvement in the Decision-Making for the Sustainable Development of the Cockpit Country, Jamaica" (Master's thesis, State University of New York, Syracuse, 2009), 57; Barbara Klamon Kopytoff, "Colonial Treaty as Sacred Charter of the Jamaican Maroons," *Ethnohistory* 26, no. 1 (1979): 57, 58; Kopytoff, "Maroons of Jamaica," 139, 145.

47. Kopytoff, "Maroons of Jamaica," 161.

48. Kopytoff, "Maroons of Jamaica," 164; Kopytoff, "Colonial Treaty," 45.

49. Kopytoff, "Maroons of Jamaica," 164.

50. Ibid., 167.

51. Kopytoff, "Jamaican Maroon Political Organization," 96; Kenneth M. Bilby, "Maroon Autonomy in Jamaica," *Cultural Survival Quarterly* 25, no. 4 (2002), 2.

52. Kopytoff, "Maroons of Jamaica," 161, 170.

53. Bilby, "Maroon Autonomy in Jamaica," 3.

54. Gad J. Heuman, *The Killing Time: The Morant Bay Rebellion in Jamaica* (Knoxville: Univ. of Tennessee Press, 1994).

55. Bilby, "Maroon Autonomy in Jamaica," 4.

56. In the literature, there are significant works on the general culture and traditions of the Maroon communities. In 2005, Kenneth Bilby published the much anticipated work *True-Born Maroons*, which explores the history and focuses on the Maroons' culture. Bilby is the most renowned expert on Jamaican Maroon communities and has worked in their communities since the late 1970s. He uses the Maroons' narrative to both verify and challenge colonial archives. The book significantly uses Maroon voices in relaying views on how they were able to defeat the British. The work is an "ethnography of identity," going into great detail on how the Maroons culturally distinguish themselves from other Jamaicans. The work also gives significant attention to narratives about Nanny, Jamaica's only female national hero. He also explores Maroons' connections to Africa. The work finally looks at the Maroon position in present-day post-colonial Jamaica. In many ways, the work is a history of the present.

57. Bilby, "Maroon Autonomy in Jamaica," 2–3; A few works explore Maroon identity, such as Barbara Kopytoff's "The Development of Jamaican Maroon Ethnicity" (1976); Mavis Campbell's "Marronage in Jamaica: Its Origin in the Seventeenth Century" (1977); and Kenneth Bilby's "Two Sister Pikni: A Historical Tradition of Dual Ethnogenesis in Eastern Jamaica" (1984).

58. Bilby, "Maroon Autonomy in Jamaica," 4.

59. "Maroons Seek Voice in Parliament," *Jamaica Gleaner* (Kingston), March 19, 1988, 11.

60. "Maroons Staking Claim to Columbus' Gold," *Jamaica Gleaner* (Kingston), April 02, 1995.

61. Currie, interview; Cawley, interview; Rowe and Ricketts, interview.

62. Social Development Commission (SDC). *Community Profile: Accompong* (Kingston, Jamaica: SDC Research Department, 2011), 4, 13.

63. Ibid., 15.

64. Ibid., 17.

65. Reid, interview; Jean Besson, "Folk Law and Legal Pluralism in Jamaica," *The Journal of Legal Pluralism and Unofficial Law* 31, no. 43 (1999): 40; Currie, interview; Garfield Rowe, interview by author, Accompong Town, St. Elizabeth, Jamaica, January 10, 2013.

66. Ferron Williams, interview by author, Accompong Town, St. Elizabeth, Jamaica, January 7, 2012; Cawley, interview; "Maroons at Accompong," *Jamaica Gleaner* (Kingston), March 21, 1964; Rowe and Ricketts, interview.

67. Agorsah, *Maroon Heritage*; Bilby, *True-Born Maroons*; Gottlieb, *The Mother of Us All*; Harris, *The Chieftainess*; Kopytoff, "The Development of Jamaican Maroon Ethnicity;" 33; Milton C. McFarlane, *Cudjoe of Jamaica: Pioneer for Black Freedom in the New World* (Short Hills, NJ: R. Enslow, 1977).

68. Colonel Martin-Luther Wright, "Accompong Maroons of Jamaica," in *Maroon Heritage Archaeological, Ethnographic, and Historical Perspectives*, ed. E. Kofi Agorsah (Barbados: Canoe Press, 1994), 70.

69. For further readings on Maroon belief systems, see the following works. Kopytoff's "Religious Change Among the Jamaican Maroons: The Ascendance of the Christian God Within a Traditional Cosmology" (1987) explores the early co-existence of Maroon cosmology and Christianity, then the later and eventual confrontation that caused the ascendance of Christianity in the early twentieth century. Ernestine Galloway's "Religious Beliefs and Practices of Maroon Children of Jamaica" (1981) mainly looks at Maroon children's religious beliefs and practices, primarily of Accompong Town. Emmanuel Obasare' s dissertation, "Implications of Jamaican Maroon Understanding of Ancestors: An Interpretation" (2005), describes the historical development of Maroon ancestral beliefs and practices. He argues that their beliefs and practices could be used to develop their communities. Other readings on Maroon belief systems include Ann B. McIver's dissertation, "The Evolution of Belief Systems and Religious Practices Among the Maroons of Accompong, Jamaica" (1978); Sultana Afroz's "From Moors to Marronage: the Islamic Heritage of the Maroons in Jamaica" (1999) and "The Manifestation of Tawhid: The Muslim Heritage of the Maroons in Jamaica" (1999); and Bilby's "The Kromanti Dance of Windward Maroons."

2
Black Abjection

> We know that the Spanish and the British called us wild and untamed savages but Maroons are freedom fighters.
>
> —Lawrence Rowe of Accompong Town Maroon Community[1]

Introduction

THE IDEA OF BLACK ABJECTION is important in the formation of the African Diaspora. In fact, abjection played an important role in the turn of the Jamaican Maroons (and others of African descent) to African Diaspora politics. Black abjection is fundamentally what peoples of African descent resist in a global order that is infused with white supremacist ideology. The European's bid to dehumanize peoples of African descent and expel them from the realm of humanity produces black abjection through racialization. Mindful of colonial abuse and the language used to support black abjection and subjugation, both the physical and the epistemological erasure that African descendants and Maroon polities have confronted will be highlighted. First, there is a brief explanation of what abjection is. The second section offers a survey of the various attempts to dehumanize African descendants in general and Maroons in particular. The last section underscores Maroon struggles for political self-determination against the dehumanizing philosophy that underpins this system, particularly the prevailing early modern European political philosophical thought, articulated by the thinkers such as Thomas Hobbes and John Locke, which works to deny these autonomous communities their political right to existence.

Abjection

Abjection is the state of being cast off or cast away.[2] According to Julia Kristeva, abjection disturbs the consensus that supports systems and social order.[3] Because of this, abject peoples, who are cast out, are not fully accepted as part of humanity in a given order. As Anne McClintock writes, "the abject is everything that the subject seeks to expunge in order to become social."[4] Furthermore, she maintains, abjection is a formative aspect of the world order where "certain groups are expelled and obliged to inhabit the impossible edges of modernity."[5] In the modern era, in order to consolidate their domination, certain peoples seek to cast others from the realm of humanity. At the same time, the dominant groups reject but cannot do without certain abject peoples, such as the enslaved and colonized peoples.[6] These attempts at expulsion or rejection are incomplete, but they work to put the peoples who are abject in a subordinate position in the current global order.

In particular, black abjection occurs through the European's endeavors to banish African peoples from the domains of humanity. In the European's bid to define itself, it sought to expel certain peoples from the human family, making Africans "black." It is racialized blackness as abjection. Darieck Scott, in *Extravagant Abjection*, engaging Frantz Fanon, states that blackness is an invention that accomplishes the domination of those who bear it as an identity.[7] Furthermore, following Fanon, Scott argues that "one becomes black in order to be subjugated by a conqueror who, in creating you as black, becomes white; blackness is both the mark and the means of subjugation."[8] In this invention, Africa becomes the site of the uncivilized and the subhuman. In this sense, all deeds and acts that deny Africans, directly or indirectly, full humanity are black abjection. It is the denial of full humanity to Africans that makes enslavement (as well as colonization and genocide) not only acceptable but justifiable, politically sanctioned, and morally endorsed. The very act of enslaving African peoples was one of the earliest bids to remove those who are blackened from humanity by making them property.

In theory and practice, African peoples are abjects of humanity by Europeans in the white supremacist global order. To concur with Percy Hintzen and Jean Muteba Rahier, the ruling ideology of white supremacy is the main force in the process of black abjection, exclusion, and erasure.[9] Fundamentally, the term "black abjection" refers to diverse states of apparent and actual disempowerment of African peoples in the modern global system.[10]

Black abjection is what the critical practice of Diaspora resists and struggles against. The voices of black abjection are presented in and by eyewitnesses, newspapers, researchers, and colonial and state authorities in the early modern era. There is a struggle over the meaning of Africa, which in the worldview of Europe tends to signify a space of the uncivilized and the savage. This worldview has legitimized the historical denial of Africans and Maroons' demand for sovereignty as an autonomous people in the Americas. It denies the capacity of Maroons' agency. Western literature is filled with accounts of Maroons living in the "state of nature" that render them abjects.

These European voices of the abjection of black people are part of the ideological struggle over the meaning of Maroons. In highlighting this issue, the anthropologists Jean and John Comaroff point to the role of Western ideas in eyewitness accounts and other stories of the African.

> [I]t is often the telling that is as significant as the tale itself. The profound forces that motivated them, and the varied vehicles of their awareness, emerge not so much from the content of those stories as from their poetics; that is, from their unselfconscious play on signs and symbols, their structures and silences, their implicit references.[11]

In such European voices, one can search for unconscious and unintentional slips that provide clues to the real meaning and intention of the source's words.[12] They show what Maroons are challenging specifically and what black people in general are resisting.

Colonial Societies

The voices of black abjection stem from eminent individuals and colonial authorities in Jamaican society and beyond. Their views are then enacted to deny peoples of African descent, including Maroons, humanity and sovereignty.

Some of the earliest accounts of abjection of the Maroons came through European narrations. In the mid-eighteenth century, one of the first detailed discussions of the Jamaican Maroons was written by a Jamaican merchant, James Knight. He considered the Maroons to be a mixture of "runaway slaves" of the Spanish, followed by other Africans who later joined them after British colonization. His description of the Maroons is accompanied by his reference to their primarily "Cromantine" origin as "bloody minded" and "murderous."[13]

One of the most influential European families in Jamaica was the Longs. Edward Long was a slaveholder, writer, judge, and politician (member of the

Jamaican Assembly), also considered one of the prominent intellectuals of the eighteenth century.[14] Long continued and expanded on the writings of Knight.[15] Long expressed a similar sentiment to Knight about the savagery of the Maroons. In Long's *The History of Jamaica*, published in 1774, his racist perspective and abjection of Africans are clear, as he considers them to be sub-humans and extensively compares them to apes, more like beasts than men.[16] According to Long, "it is better that the Negroe should continue as an honest and industrious slave, than to be turned into an idle and profligate freedman."[17] Furthermore, he contends:

> We might reasonably suppose, that the commerce maintained with the Europeans for above two centuries, and the great variety of fabrics and things manufactured, which have been introduced among the Guiney Negroes for such a length of time, might have wrought some effect towards polishing their manners, and exciting in them at least a degree of imitative industry; but it is really astonishing to find, that these causes have not operated to their civilization; they are at this day, if any credit can be given to the most modern accounts, but little divested of their primitive brutality; we cannot pronounce them insusceptible of civilization, since even apes have been taught to eat, drink, repose, and dress, like men; but of all human species hitherto discovered, their natural baseness of mind seems to afford the least hope.[18]

As a legislator and judge with these views, Long was able to create laws and enforce them to abject Africans and Maroons.

Another influential Jamaican family was the Edwards'. According to Bryan Edwards, a slaveholder, merchant, and politician, Africans and Maroons were barbarians and savages. An ardent racist, he was a secretary for the Association for Promoting the Discovery of the Interior Parts of Africa.[19] William Wilberforce, the abolitionist, considered Edwards one of his strongest opponents. As a friend of the Scottish explorer Mungo Park, Edwards used this connection to defend his racist views of the barbarity of Africans. As a member of the Jamaican Assembly and later Member of Parliament of England, he used his position to implement his racist views and abjection of Africans throughout the British Empire. [20]

In his *An Historical Survey of the Island of Saint Domingo Together with an Account of the Maroon Negroes in the Island of Jamaica*, Edwards considers Africans at the lowest degree of civilization.[21] He claims that he has had a "long experience and observation" of Maroons and has concluded that they are not fully human.[22] According to Edwards, the Jamaican Maroons are "ignorant people in civilizations and morals," and he views them as in a savage state.[23] He argues that in the Maroon villages, "I never could perceive any vestige of culture."[24]

The poet and writer Robert Charles Dallas also came from an influential Jamaican family. Unlike most other European-Jamaicans of the time, Dallas was an anti-slavery advocate.[25] He is the author of the *History of the Maroons*, published in 1803. Although sympathetic to the Maroons and generally to the enslaved African cause, he can still be seen presenting Maroons as abjects. At times siding with the previous writers about Africans, such as Long and Edwards, Dallas also refers to African descendants and Maroons as savages.[26] He restates earlier writers' references to Kojo, the Maroon leader, as a man with "strong African features" and "a peculiar wildness in his manners."[27] So, the casting of black abjection happens even with seemingly antiracist individuals.

In the British Empire, slaveholders were often the head of government of the colonial societies.[28] The colonial state was the apparatus used to rule the societies and the main mechanism used to dehumanize Maroons and other Africans. As the highest authority in the colonial government and society, governors executed the rules of the society that abjected Maroons and Africans. Edward Trelawny, who was governor when the Treaties were signed with the Maroons, believed that slavery was an unsustainable institution.[29] Nevertheless, he led a system that abjected peoples of African descent.

The colonial legislative assembly was controlled by slaveholders, such as Long and Edwards. In the slave era, it was a body that significantly focused on regulating the slave society by creating dehumanizing laws.[30] In English property law that was applied to Jamaica, domestic animals, like enslaved people, were considered chattel. Classifying enslaved people as chattel property was aligned with the idea that Africans and their descendants were more like animals than human beings.[31]

There were various acts, letters, reports, and proceedings that made abjects of Africans and Maroons in the colonial state. For instance, *The Proceedings of the Governor and Assembly of Jamaica in Regard to the Maroon Negroes: Published by Order of the Assembly*, written by Edwards on behalf of the Jamaican Assembly, draws from many earlier documents and views of the government of Jamaica. Africans are referred to as "having no moral senses" and no understanding of the laws and customs of civilized nations.[32] These proceedings, like many other documents, refer to Africans in general and Maroons in particular as savages and barbarians. [33] In fact, in the same proceedings, Edwards states that Maroons are more savage creatures than the animals such as dogs used to hunt them.[34]

In this, probably the single most relevant and damning document from the colonial legislators related to the treatment of African descendants, we find the Slave Codes (Black Codes or *Code Noir*). The point of the Codes was to regulate the rights and duties of enslaved people and how free people should treat them. The Codes tended to focus on the restriction of movement, prohibitions on gathering, and punishment and murder of enslaved people.[35] The Codes determined that slave status passed from mother to child, similar to domestic animals in England.[36] Fundamentally, the Codes, along with other laws direct and indirect, enforced black abjection.

For most of the slave era in Jamaica, the Black Codes reflected how slaveholders tried to control enslaved Africans. It was only in the late eighteenth century, impacted by the anti-slavery movement, that the Black Codes were modified to be more compassionate, to hide the true nature and desires of the slaveholders. Nevertheless, abjection of Africans is still apparent. For instance, the Slave Codes of 1789, drawn from Edward Long's Papers, titled "An Abstract of the Jamaica *Code Noir*, or Laws affecting Negroe and other Slaves in that Island.—And, first of, PENAL ARTICLES" in its very title equates slavery with people of African descent (only such people were enslaved in Jamaica at that point).[37]

Another example, in the same Code, refers to the idea that Africans thinking of murdering a white person can be executed merely for what they might have had in their mind.[38] Moreover, based on the document, "A person killing a slave in the fact of stealing, or running away, or found in the night out of his owner's or employer's estate, or on the road, and refusing to submit, such person is not liable to action or damage for the same."[39] Once again, the Code served to dehumanize Africans, who could be murdered on suspicion of resistance to the inhuman circumstance.[40]

Similar to the executive and legislative branches of the colonial government, slaveholders controlled the judicial system. The laws were inhuman to people of African descent, whether freed or enslaved. Moreover, the law provided financial rewards to anyone who killed a Maroon leader (in the pre-Treaty days).[41] The colonial state occasionally raised temporary military forces to re-enslave or kill Maroons.[42] Besides financial incentives to hunt Maroons, the colonial government allowed white men to plunder at will Maroon communities.[43] At one point, enslaved Africans were granted freedom if they killed or captured a Maroon.[44] In Jamaica, the Assembly passed forty-four laws to eliminate Maroon communities, which destroyed many such settlements.[45]

Although these laws in the later years of the slave era called for more protection of the enslaved person, the judicial system found that difficult to enforce. For the most part, the colonial government felt that the slaveholders should deal with enslaved individuals as they saw fit. With no enforcement agency to supervise the treatment of enslaved people, the treatment of enslaved individuals was in the planters' hands to do as they wished, continuing black abjection.[46]

In the judicial system of the Jamaican colony, peoples of African descent were not treated humanely. Sometimes, so-called criminal cases were tried by "slave courts" before justices and freeholders. In this, jury trials were not allowed for Africans. Also, evidence of an enslaved person was admitted against other enslaved individuals and liberated Africans (Maroons) but not against white people.[47]

In the legal system, Africans were abject. The enforcement of these laws included a wide range of punishments, including death. In the early eighteenth century, Hans Sloane described the punishment of enslaved Africans who resisted slavery:

> The Punishments for Crimes of Slaves, are usually for Rebellions burning them, by nailing them down on the ground with crooked sticks on every Limb and then applying the Fire by degrees from the Feet and Hands, burning them gradually up to the Head, whereby their pains are extravagant. For Crimes of a lesser nature Gelding, or chopping off half of the Foot with an Ax. These Punishments are suffered by them with great Constancy.
>
> For running away they put Iron Rings of great weight on their Ankles, or Pottocks about their Necks, which are Iron Rings with two long Necks rivetted to them, or a Spur in the Mouth.[48]

This description highlights that some of the harsher punishments were inflicted on enslaved people trying to escape slavery.[49] Many recaptured Maroons often faced torture and death. They were hunted and often murdered, with the colonial state rewarding perpetrators of these heinous acts. The inhuman treatment of African-descended peoples in colonial society is still remembered today through oral tradition among the Maroons and other black Jamaicans. The anthropologist Kenneth Bilby recounts oral tradition in songs of horrible acts against people of African descent, such as being buried alive.

Local and International Press

Throughout the more than three-hundred-year-long colonial era of Jamaica, the press, local and international, disseminated an image of black people, particularly Maroons, that framed them as subhuman, justifying inferior status and poor treatment. The Western press in Jamaica presented Maroons' origin as an indication of their savagery. For the most part, in this period, this origin was cited only generally as Africa, with associated ideas of primitiveness, but often with no details of specific locations. In the late nineteenth century, it did become more popular, at times, to identify the specific place of origin of the Maroons, although Africa in general was still emphasized.

The newspapers of colonial Jamaica, including the *Royal Gazette*, *The Diary and Kingston Daily Advertiser*, and *Jamaica Courant*, represented views of the white slaveholders and planters such as Edwards, Knight, and Long.[50] However, the *Gleaner* of Jamaica is the local press that has given the most attention to the Maroons. The paper was founded in 1834 and continues to operate today. In the post-emancipation era up to Jamaica's independence in the newspaper, dozens of times people of African descent, including Maroons, were referred to as savages, barbarians, or primitives.[51] For instance, in 1937 in an article titled "Jamaican Tribe Emerges as Tourists Visit the Island," it is said of Maroons: "They have been free twice as long as the other blacks of Jamaica, but their liberty has been that of a savage tribe."[52] Even in the post-colonial era, in the mid-1990s, it was said that Maroons were "known as primitive bush people and forever will be patronized by the rest of Jamaica and the world."[53] Even though Africans through marronage liberated themselves from slavery, their achievements are undermined in dehumanizing terms. It was only in post-colonial Jamaica that such negative language about the Maroons has been largely abandoned.

Other periodicals abjected people of African descent and Maroons.[54] The *Port Folio*, a Philadelphian literary and political magazine published in the early nineteenth century, in a piece titled "Tour Through Jamaica," refers to Maroons as "wild men" and very warlike.[55] The *Atheneum* (London, England), in an article written by J. Steward titled "Interesting Notes on Jamaica," refers to Maroons as savages and barbaric people.[56] It further expresses the idea that enslaved Africans do not "wish to return, had they it even in their power, to their original wild life and savage state of precarious liberty" in Africa.[57] In *Macmillan's Magazine*, a monthly British magazine of the late nineteenth and early twentieth century, a piece titled "Rebellion in the West Indies" explains to their readers that Maroons' origins are as "hog-hunters" and "wild negroes" who "lived in indolent savagery while their provisions lasted, and in active brigandage when their wants forced them to plunder. They were fond of blood and barbarity, as is the nature of savages, and never spared a prisoner, black or white."[58] Another example, in 1866, in *Every Saturday: A Journal of Choice Reading*, an American literary magazine, an article titled "The Maroons of Jamaica" acknowledges Maroons' origin in Africa but considers them to be "principally those imported from the Coromantee country, on the coast of Africa, a people inured to savage warfare."[59] Once again, Maroons are linked to savagery. In 1898, *Harper's Magazine* referred to the Maroons as "mongrel looking" and having undesirable "mental traits unmistakabl[y] African."[60] In short, Western cultures dehumanized Africans through negative characterizations of the enslaved and those that liberated themselves from slavery as primitives, savages, and barbarians.

Political Philosophical Underpinning

In turn, Africans re-asserted their humanity through many different means, marronage being one of the most viable formations to oppose enslavement and colonialism. However, even as Maroons established their own communities, the West still attempted to cast Africans out of the realm of humanity. The prevailing early modern Western political and philosophical thought underpinned this worldview and gave support to individuals and institutions in Europe, the Americas, and other parts of the globe where Western influence was felt.

Early modern Western political philosophers have devoted insufficient time to studying political organizations that do not fit the profile of a Western state. Many of these philosophers have basically called for the destruction of other means of political organizing, often leading to the foreclosure of the possibility of alternative forms of political organizing. Going further, the dominant political ideological views and acts have destroyed a sizeable segment of the world population that follows alternative political organizational forms.

Western political philosophers have privileged the organizing of peoples into particular kinds of states over any other forms, and this approach has shaped ideas about what constitutes acceptable forms of political organization in Europe, the Americas, and all over the world. In *On Sovereignty,* Jean Bodin declared that while others are "prompted to distinguish more than three kinds of state," he continued to believe that only three types are really worth considering.[61] Niccolò Machiavelli, in *The Prince*, insists that "All states, all forms of government that have had, and continue to have authority over men, have been, and are either republics or principalities."[62] Other political philosophers, such as Thomas Hobbes and John Locke, went further by comparing a state of nature and the state (or commonwealth).

Of these two philosophers, Hobbes, writing in the seventeenth century, had the most detailed description of the state of nature, which is the foundation for the social contract. To Hobbes, men are in a state of nature when they are "without a common power to keep them all in awe."[63] In this state, according to Hobbes, human beings are basically equal.[64] Also, in the state of nature, men are inhibited only by physical obstacles and are in a state of complete liberty. However, the state of nature has another side. According to the philosopher, men "are in that condition [state of nature] which is called war, and such a war as is of every man against every man. For war consisteth not in battle only, or the act of fighting, but in a tract of time wherein the will to contend by battle is sufficiently known."[65] In the state of nature, there is no uniform justice or injustice (and right or wrong).[66] Men's lives are "solitary, poor, nasty, brutish and short."[67]

There have been questions about whether or not the state of nature actually exists or has ever existed. Is it an experimental thought, historical reality, or present condition of human beings?[68] In some sense, the response is yes to all the points of this question. The state of nature, as the philosopher A. P. Martinich concurs, is a heuristic device that Hobbes employs to explain the need for the state and to justify its existence.[69] Also, according to Hobbes, "It may peradventure be thought, there was never such a time nor condition of war as this; and I believe it was never generally so, over all the world."[70] However, Hobbes makes reference to the presence of savage peoples who were living in the state of nature in the Americas during the seventeenth century.[71] Hobbes might have had indigenous peoples of the Americas in mind, but he could also have been referring to Maroon societies (regardless of their form of political organization). Indeed, as the philosopher Edwin Curley succinctly states, in his introduction to Hobbes' *Leviathan*, "When Hobbes talks about the state of nature, he is not necessarily talking about the prehistoric condition of the human race, or what life was like in the primitive societies of his day, or about a condition which is merely a theoretical possibility. He is talking about any situation where there is no effective government to impose order."[72] In the end, regardless of all of these three thoughts, Maroon communities were considered to be in the state of nature, and therefore ought not to exist and should be destroyed (not recognizing that these communities did have an "effective government to impose order" because it was a non-Western one).

John Locke views the state of nature as not being as harsh as Hobbes describes, but for him it is still not an ideal state. According to Locke, the state of nature is a state that all men are naturally in.[73] In *The Second Treatise of Government*, Locke mentions that the state of nature "is a state of perfect freedom" for men "to order their actions and dispose of their possessions and persons as they think fit, within the bonds of the law of nature, without asking leave, or depending upon the will of any other man." It is a state of equality among men, with no one generally having more power than another. Furthermore, Locke declares that "though this be a state of liberty, yet it is not a state of license, though man in that state have an uncontrollable liberty to dispose of his person or possessions, yet he has not liberty to destroy himself, or so much as any creature in his possession, but where some nobler use than its bare preservation calls for it."[74] Locke believes that in the state of nature one is exposed to the state of war, which is "a state of enmity and destruction," where if a man has designs upon another man's life it "puts him in a state of war with him against whom he has declared such an intention."[75] The enjoyment of rights in the state of nature is uncertain, with continual exposure to the invasion of others. Indeed, the enjoyment of the property one has in this state is unsafe and insecure. This condition where man is free is also full of fears and unremitting dangers.

Many early modern political philosophers, especially Hobbes and Locke, besides privileging a particular kind of state/commonwealth, call for or accept the idea of direct violence against and complete destruction of peoples who are deemed to exist in the state of nature. For Hobbes, one does not even really count as a people until they are represented in a legal way under a particular kind of government, which means that Maroon societies are unrecognized entities and subject to destruction.[76] In Locke's eyes, men who are not in the state "are not under the ties of the common law of reason, have no other rule but that of force and violence, and so may be treated as beasts of prey, those dangerous and noxious creatures, that will be sure to destroy him whenever he falls into their power."[77] These "creatures" must be murdered before they murder you.

Maroon communities challenge the dichotomy between the state and the state of nature, a notion that is fundamental to social contract theories for explaining and describing human political organization. These communities complicate the prevailing political philosophical thought that lumps various and distinctive political formations into the state of nature. Maroon communities contest this idea that is the basis for the morally justifiable destruction of countless other societies, cultures, and peoples.

Conclusion

Black abjection is embedded in the structures of all colonies in the Western Hemisphere. It was apparent in the words and deeds of European nations' eminent members as they created colonies in the Americas and beyond. Particularly, it was instituted in the colonial state apparatus: the executive, legislative, and judicial systems. It manifested itself in the major publications of the times—especially in the local and international press. Most significantly, the abjection of Maroon and black communities has been systematically implemented and institutionalized in colonial states and societies through acceptance of the prevailing early modern Western philosophical thought. These foundational acts that were introduced in the colonial era can be felt in all of the post-colonial societies of the Americas.

Black abjection, particularly in the form of racialization, continues today. It is exhibited in the many different ways in which black people face social, economic, and political exclusion. It is made apparent when and where African-descended people's humanity is not fully recognized, both in Jamaica and worldwide.

Notes

1. Lawrence Rowe and Lance Ricketts, interview by author, Accompong Town, St. Elizabeth, Jamaica, January 8, 2012.
2. *Merriam-Webster.com Dictionary*, s.v. "abjection," accessed March 26, 2020, https://www.merriam-webster.com/dictionary/abjection; Imogen Tyler, *Revolting Subjects: Social Abjection and Resistance in Neoliberal Britain* (London: Zed Books Ltd, 2013), 20.
3. Julia Kristeva, *Powers of Horror: An Essay of Abjection* (New York: Columbia University Press, 1984), 4.
4. Ann MacClintock, *Imperial Leather: Race, Gender and Sexuality in Colonial Context* (New York: Routledge, 1995), 71.
5. Ibid., 72.
6. Ibid.
7. Darieck Scott, *Extravagant Abjection: Blackness, Power, and Sexuality in the African American Literary Imagination* (New York: New York University Press, 2016), 4.
8. Ibid., 38.
9. Percy C. Hintzen and Jean Muteba Rahier, "Introduction," in *Global Circuits of Blackness: Interrogating the African Diaspora*, eds. Jean Muteba Rahier, Percy C. Hintzen, and Felipe Smith (Urbana: University of Illinois Press, 2010), x.
10. Scott, *Extravagant Abjection*, 15.
11. Jean Comaroff and John L. Comaroff, *Of Revelation and Revolution: Christianity, Colonialism, and Consciousness in South Africa, Vol.1*, (Chicago: University of Chicago Press, 1991), 36.
12. Ibid.; Willie Thompson, *Postmodernism and History* (Basingstoke [Hampshire]: Palgrave Macmillan, 2004), 124.
13. Edward Long, "The History of Jamaica to 1742," 1746, file 12416, Edward Long Papers [Microfilm], Butler Library, Columbia University, New York, NY.
14. Devin Leigh, "The Origin of a Source: Edward Long, Coromantee Slave Revolts and The History of Jamaica," *Slavery & Abolition* 40, no. 2 (2019): 299.
15. Edward Long, *The History of Jamaica, or, General Survey of the Antient and Modern State of the Island: With Reflections on Its Situation Settlements, Inhabitants, Climate, Products, Commerce, Laws, and Government: Illustrated with Copper Plates, Vol. I, II, & III* (London: T. Lowndes, 1774).
16. Long, *The History of Jamaica, Vol II*, 361, 364.
17. Ibid., 323.

18. Ibid., 376.

19. "Edwards, Bryan," *The History of Parliament Online*, accessed March 27, 2020, http://www.historyofparliamentonline.org/volume/1790-1820/member/edwards-bryan-1743-1800.

20. Ibid.

21. Bryan Edwards, *The History, Civil and Commercial, of the British Colonies in the West Indies: in two volumes. By Bryan Edwards, Esq. of the island of Jamaica; F.R.S.S.A. and member of the American Philosophical Society at Philadelphia* (London: Printed for John Stockdale, 1794), 320.

22. Ibid., 327.

23. Ibid., 318–319, 321.

24. Ibid., 321.

25. Michael Ashcroft, "Robert Charles Dallas: Identified as the Author of an Anonymous Book About Jamaica," *Jamaica Journal* no. 44 (1979): 96–98.

26. Robert Charles Dallas, *The History of the Maroons, from Their Origin to the Establishment of Their Chief Tribe at Sierra Leone* (London: T. N. Longman and O. Rees, 1803), 45, 73.

27. Ibid., 53.

28. Edward Bartlett Rugemer, *Slave Law and the Politics of Resistance in the Early Atlantic World* (Cambridge, MA: Harvard University Press, 2018), 2.

29. Ibid., 158.

30. Ibid., 2.

31. Ibid., 50.

32. Bryan Edwards, *The Proceedings of the Governor and Assembly of Jamaica, in Regard to the Maroon Negroes: Published by Order of the Assembly. [Reprinted.] To Which Is Prefixed an Introductory Account [by B. Edwards] Containing Observations on the Disposition . . . and Habits of Life, of the Maroons, and a Detail . . . of the Late War between Those People and the White Inhabitants* (London, Government Publication, 1796), i–ii.

33. Ibid., iii, iv, lxxx, and lxxxix.

34. Ibid., lxviii.

35. Robert Worthington Smith, "The Legal Status of Jamaican Slaves Before the Anti-Slavery Movement," *The Journal of Negro History* 30, no. 3 (1945): 296.

36. Rugemer, *Slave Laws and the Politics of Resistance*, 50.

37. Edward Long, "An Abstract of the Jamaica *Code Noir*, or Laws affecting Negroe and other Slaves in that Island.—And, first of, PENAL ARTICLES," 1746, File 12416, Edward Long Papers [Microfilm], Butler Library, Columbia University, New York, NY, 485.

38. Ibid., 486.

39. Ibid., 488.

40. Rugemer, *Slave Laws and the Politics of Resistance*, 36.

41. Ibid., 39 and 40.

42. Ibid., 120.

43. Ibid., 127.

44. Ibid., 129.

45. Ibid., 154.

46. Smith, "The Legal Status of Jamaican Slaves," 296, 302.

47. Ibid., 297.

48. Hans Sloane, *A Voyage to the Islands Madera, Barbados, Nieves, S. Christophers and Jamaica With the Natural History of the Herbs and Trees, Four-Footed Beasts, Fishes, Birds, Insects, Reptiles, &C. of the Last of Those Islands; to Which Is Prefix'd an Introduction, Wherein Is an Account of the Inhabitants, Air, Waters, Diseases, Trade, &C. of That Place, with Some Relations Concerning the Neighbouring Continent, and Islands of America. Illustrated with the Figures of the Things Describ'd, Which Have Not Been Heretofore Engraved; In Large Copper-Plates As Big As the Life. By Hans Sloane, M. D. Fellow of the College of Physicians and Secretary of the Royal-Society. In Two Volumes, Vol. I,* (London, BM: 1707), lvii.

49. Mavis Christine Campbell, *The Maroons of Jamaica: 1655–1796* (Trenton, NJ: Africa World Press, 1990), 10.

50. Michael Sivapragasam, "After the Treaties: A Social, Economic and Demographic History of Maroon Society in Jamaica, 1739–1842" (PhD diss., Southampton University, 2018), 279.

51. "Jamaican Tribe Emerges as Tourists Visit the Island," *Daily Gleaner* (Kingston), January 26, 1937, 27; Simon Harcourt-Smith, "The Maroons: Their Quiet Self-Assurance and Pure English," *Daily Gleaner* (Kingston), May 7, 1964, 3; "A Canadian Opinion of Jamaica," *Daily Gleaner* (Kingston), December 19, 1888, 7; "Jamaica: A Paradise Without a Passport," *Sunday Gleaner* (Kingston), Jan. 6, 1947, 6.

52. "Jamaican Tribe," 27.

53. "Leadership row set to hit Maroon celebrations," *Jamaica Gleaner* (Kingston), January 6, 1993, 1.

54. "The Maroons of Jamaica," *Every Saturday: A Journal of Choice Reading (1866–1874)*, January 13, 1866, 51.

55. "Tour Through Jamaica," *The Port – Folio*, October 1812, 368.

56. J. Steward, "Interesting Notes on Jamaica," *The Atheneum*, November 15, 1823, 152.

57. Ibid., 164.

58. J. W. Fortescue, "Rebellion in the West Indies," *Macmillan's Magazine*, November 1, 1894, 73, 74 and 79.

59. "Maroons of Jamaica," 50.

60. Phil Robinson, "The Maroons of Jamaica," *Harper's Weekly*, October 29, 1898, 3.

61. Jean Bodin, *On Sovereignty: Four Chapters from the Six Books of the Commonwealth*, ed. Julian H. Franklin (Cambridge [England]: Cambridge University Press, 1992), 89–90.

62. Niccolò Machiavelli, *Selected Political Writings*, trans. David Wootton (Indianapolis: Hackett Pub. Co, 1994), 6.

63. Thomas Hobbes, *Leviathan: With Selected Variants from the Latin Edition of 1668*, ed. E. M. Curley (Indianapolis: Hackett Pub. Co, 1994), 76.

64. Ibid., 74.

65. Ibid., 76; John H. Hallowell and J. M. Porter, *Political Philosophy: The Search for Humanity and Order* (Scarborough, Ont: Prentice Hall Canada, 1997), 311.

66. Hobbes, *Leviathan*, 78.

67. Ibid., vii.

68. Gordon J. Schochet, "Thomas Hobbes on the Family and the State of Nature," *Political Science Quarterly* 82, no. 3 (September 1967), 431–32; Richard Ashcraft, "Hobbes's Natural Man: A Study in Ideology Formation," *The Journal of Politics* 33, no. 4 (November 1971): 1109.

69. A. P. Martinich, *Thomas Hobbes* (London: Macmillan Publishers Limited, 1996), 63, 292.

70. Hobbes, *Leviathan*, 77.

71. Robert P. Kraynak, "Hobbes on Barbarism and Civilization," *The Journal of Politics* 45, No. 1 (1983): 90.

72. Hobbes, *Leviathan*, xxi.

73. John Locke, *Political Writings*, ed. David Wootton (New York, NY: Mentor, 1993), 262.

74. Ibid., 263.

75. Ibid., 269 and 324–325.

76. Kinch Hoekstra, "History of Political Thought" (lecture, University of California, Berkeley, April 02, 2009); The fact that the colonial regimes often signed treaties with Maroon communities and these communities had governing systems is not fully acknowledged by the colonial state. First, whether successful or not, these colonial powers are signing treaties and attempting to accept these Maroon societies' existence under the assumption that they will be incorporated as a non-sovereign community within the colonial state. Second, although maroon communities have a government, the colonial state does not recognize them as such.

77. Locke, *Political Writings*, 269.

3
Origin

> One of the things that people need to bear in mind is that the history of our foreparents did not start the day they stepped off the slave ships, on the shores of these islands. The history of our foreparents started thousands of years before, when they were living in Africa.
>
> —Colonel Wallace Sterling of Moore Town Maroon Community[1]

Introduction

THE IDEA OF COMMON ORIGIN is vital in understanding the critical practice, articulation, and politics of Diaspora.[2] Maroons make distinctive claims of origin as a means of anchoring and linking themselves to Africa. It is possible to examine these claims through Maroon voices, with an emphasis on their language and methods of enunciating the claims. In a hostile New World environment, origin emerged as a significant response and resistance to black abjection. It was black abjection, probably more than anything else, that made African descendants turn to origin. In this, one can identify and scrutinize what Maroons have deemed to be of African origin in the intangible and tangible cultural expressions of their communities. A nuanced look at the expression of these claims illustrates the ideological struggle and resistance of the Maroons against Western worldviews on the abjection of Africans.

The Maroons' view of their origin is a critical practice and ultimately ideological, serving a number of purposes. It is used as a means of nation-building for Maroons. I agree with Paul Gilroy that the acquisition of roots is needed to create a political agenda in which the ideal of rootedness is identified as a prerequisite for the forms of cultural integrity that could guarantee the nationhood to which people aspire.[3] More significantly, it serves as a source of identity and culture politics of displaced, enslaved, and colonized people.[4] The critical practice serves as a means to resist the Western narrative of black abjection, contesting the foreclosure of Africans as modern subjects and their location on the constitutive outside of the civilized state.

Oral Histories

Maroons, like other people of African descent, make claims to origin in Africa—a critical practice with ideological significance. Often, Maroons' enunciation of claims of origin is a means of giving language to present preoccupations through a particular kind of representation of the past. As Stuart Hall rightly states, "language is the medium par excellence through which things are represented in thought and thus the medium in which ideology is generated and transformed."[5] In many respects, the Maroons' claims of origin are central tenets in shaping their ideological view. Here, employing Hall's definition, I am viewing ideology as consisting of the "mental frameworks—the languages, the concepts, categories, imagery of thought, and the systems of representation—which different classes and social groups deploy in order to make sense of, define, figure out and render intelligible" the way the world works.[6] Hence, an examination of the Maroons' enunciation of origin reveals the significance and power of their ideological view and critical practice, as we will explore.

An optimal way to capture Maroon voices (phenomenologically) is through their oral histories. As a form of collective historical memory, oral histories tell the story of where a group of people comes from and how they should act in the present and even the future. Oral histories allow the research subjects' understanding, meaning, and interpretation to be (re)presented as valid. They acknowledge that social reality is mediated through meaning and symbolic communication rather than claims to "objective" and concrete "facts." This does not mean that the concrete and the objective are unimportant; rather, it reveals that the interpretation of them is even more important.

Maroons have a long history of asserting claims to origin in Africa.[7] Even during the British colonial period, such claims were emphasized. As the leader of Accompong Maroon community, Colonel H. A. Rowe (1920–c. 1943), stated in the 1930s: "the Maroons have no Arawak blood in them—the Maroons are pure negroes," thus claiming solely African origin.[8] Here, there is a rejection of hybridity and hybrid origin. At that time, the reference to "pure" was to signal and challenge the idea of "mongrel" origin. But Maroons' critical practice now resists this characterization and imposition.

Maroons have articulated claims to African origin in an even more pronounced way in the post-colonial era of Jamaican history. In the 1990s, according to former Colonel Martin-Luther Wright (1967–1984 and 1988–1993), Accompong Maroons traced their origins to both Arawak Indians and Africans who escaped Spanish and English domination to establish independent communities.[9] He further states of the Maroons: "They continue to practice and enjoy traditional customs handed down by our American and, particularly, African guerrilla ancestors."[10] As with some other Maroon views, origin here is acknowledged as hybrid, but Africa is centrally positioned as the most important root. Hence, I am arguing that although the Maroons acknowledge origin outside of Africa, the latter is afforded a privileged position.

Some Maroons argue that African presence in Jamaica preceded slavery and colonialism and coincided with the initial Europeans' encounter with the New World. The former Colonel Harris Cawley (1984–1988) traces the Maroons' origin to two continents—Africa and Europe—but privileges African origin. He observes that people originally from Africa who went to Europe as well as those who came directly from the African continent were both sites of the Maroons' origin:

> The Maroons were among the first Africans that came to the islands under the Spanish. Because you know in Spain, they have a lot of Africans. So, when Christopher Columbus was exploring the Caribbean, a lot of Africans came with him, and they were the hard type of people. So afterwards, the Spanish started to import them from Africa to work on the plantation. They were the first ones who came in to inhabit the land, after the Arawaks, and they have lived here for 461 years after the British took over in 1655.[11]

Thus, according to former Colonel Cawley, the early Maroons who originated in Europe were actually Africans, many of whom had formerly served in the courts of Spain.[12] Former Colonel Frank Lumsden (2004–2015) of Charles Town Maroon community and other Maroons also believe many of the Maroons originated in Spain before being joined by West Africans. In this view, Maroons are emphasizing and signaling African origin in great civilizations not only in Africa but in Europe as well. Most importantly, Maroons' claims to territory began at the exact time of the European conquest. The implication is that the original African presence was constituted by free and modern subjects rather than un-free and enslaved ones.

The claims to African origin reference multiple locations on the continent and, as we have just seen, even pre-colonial African presence in Europe. In many instances, the identification of a specific place in Africa is introduced in evidence as the point of origin on the continent: that the details prove the claims of African origin and highlight deep roots in the continent. It must be noted, however, that in highlighting certain groups, Maroons do not deny the existence of the dozens of other possible groups. Let us examine the details of these claims, which ultimately further ideological struggle and critical practice about the meaning and significance of origin in Africa.

Various Maroon individuals have expressed the view about roots in Africa or specific African groups. Some refer to specific African groups such as Akan, Igbo, or Kongolese, to which they are directly linked. For example, Maroons make ethnic and cultural claims to these groups in their various oral histories, including references to artifacts.

In Accompong Town, their oral histories stress Asante, Kromanti (often associated with the Akan peoples of the Gold Coast), and Kongo origin. The Maroon historian and Deputy Colonel Melville Currie also asserted that Accompong Maroons came from various African groups, especially the Asante, Kromanti, and Kongo peoples. After the Africans left the plantations to go to the hills, they separated themselves into "tribal" groups, just as they were in Africa. He said that is why there are different burial grounds in Accompong Town, where each group of people buried their own dead.[13] Kojo, Nanny, and Accompong (Akyeampong), three of the most influential historic Maroon leaders, are cited as being Asante or Kromanti (or Akan, as explained later) by most Maroons. In present-day Accompong Town, there is a particular burial ground where the Asante, Kromanti, and Kongo ancestors were laid to rest.

The prominent tour guide Lawrence Rowe claims that the Maroons' origins are in different African groups, including the Asante, Kongo, Igbo, Kromanti, Mandingo, and Yoruba.[14] Lawrence believes that the Kromantis were the largest group of Africans among the early Accompong Maroons. As a tour guide, he regularly shows visitors the Asante, Kromanti, and Kongo burial ground as an example of the groups' presence among the early Maroons.[15] According to Rowe and other community members, there are currently different groups of African peoples living in different parts of their settlement. He cites how the Kongo people and their descendants have lived toward the northeastern end of the community.[16] Rowe describes the Kongo people as being short and stocky. He says that when most of the Kongo people came from Africa, they lived at a place in the community called "Creep Up."[17] Rowe considers the Asante, in contrast, to be physically bigger and fearless.[18] At the annual Maroon Independence Day celebration (also referred to as Kojo Day and Sixth of January) in Accompong Town, which I witnessed in 2012, 2013, 2015, and 2018, the three main groups—Asante, Kromanti, and Kongo—were highlighted the most in the public presentations about Maroon origin.

The Windward Maroons—of Moore Town, Charles Town, and Scot's Hall—highlight their Kromanti origin. Kromanti is also mentioned as one of the major groups that Kojo employed in his battles against the British. In 1977, Milton MacFarlane, a Moore Town Maroon, published a work titled *Cudjoe of Jamaica*, in which he states that Kojo's father, Prince Naquan, was born to the Koromanteen (Kromanti) house and Kojo was brought up in the proud and strict tradition of those people. McFarlane remarks that Kojo's father "taught him all about the homeland in West Africa and the lives of the Koromanteens."[19] MacFarlane goes on:

> Almost all the Africans brought to the British West Indies were shipped from ports on the west coast of the [African] continent, particularly Nigeria and the Gold Coast (present-day Ghana). The first English fort on the Gold Coast, in 1631, was at Kromantine, and this name in various forms was later applied to all slaves from the Gold Coast, who were in the majority. Most of the names of the Maroon leaders—Cudjoe [Kojo], Accompong, Quacu, Kishee, Quao—are versions of common names among the Akan peoples of Ghana.[20]

In fact, the names Kromanti, Kormanti, and Coromantee refer to not an ethnic group of Africans, but African captives who embarked from the fort of Kormantine (around Kormantse, Ghana) and some other forts or castles in present-day Ghana.[21] According to MacFarlane, during battles with the British in the early eighteenth century, Kojo often reflected on the easier life his forefathers had in West Africa.[22] MacFarlane further claims that during the negotiations with the British over a Peace Treaty, Kojo told the British Colonel Guthrie that the Maroons desired only to return to their home in West Africa.[23]

The point here is that in making claims to African origin, the Maroons sometimes identify a specific place in Africa as their homeland in an effort to drive that idea home. The significance is that it demonstrates how and in which manner this narrative has become central to the Maroons' construction of identity and their conscious representation of self. This distinguishes the Maroons from the rest of black Jamaican society even in practice, notwithstanding their profound similarities.

Colonel Wallace Sterling (1995–present) of Moore Town argues that the Maroons' origin is indeed in Africa and emphasizes the significance of the Asante, but also Amerindian roots:

> One of the things that people need to bear in mind is that the history of our foreparents did not start the day they stepped off the slave ships, on the shores of these islands. The history of our foreparents started thousands of years before, when they were living in Africa. And it is also true to say that some of our foreparents were Amerindians. So, it's not that all of them were Africans: some

> of them were Amerindians. And they had a history of how they governed themselves wherever they were. Our African foreparents, because they are the more dominant ones, when they were in Africa, they pretty much had their system of government. There was a chief or a chieftainess—a ruler.[24]

Sterling is still claiming Africa as the main site of the origin of his foreparents.[25] But this claim is doing more than identifying a place of origin. It is part of the critical practice and ideological struggle positioning African civilization as ancient and powerful. It speaks to the heart of the cultural politics of representation and the struggles over meaning and recognition.

Sterling states that Nanny, like many Moore Town community members, came to Jamaica from West Africa and was from the "highly spiritual Asante tribe."[26] This is a Maroon view of modernity that challenges even the view of modernity of some Jamaicans and Westerners. As a critical practice, Africa represents a place of great significance, challenging the claims to exclusive civilized modernity by Europeans.

Bev Carey, a "Maroon descendant" (as she calls herself) of Moore Town and author of *Maroon Story*, emphasizes the Asante (and Akan) as the main ethnic group of origin but also acknowledges other African and Amerindian groups.[27]According to Carey, Maroons spoke several languages, but the most common was Kromanti, which she argues closely resembles the modern African Twi language.[28] As Carey and other Maroons rightly point out, there is no ethnic group in Africa known as Kromanti.[29] Recently, instead of referring to "Kromanti," many Maroons use the terms Akan or Asante. Carey also makes reference to knowledge about certain Maroon families in Moore Town who were described as being of Igbo, Dahomean, and West African Muslim origin.[30]

C. L. G. Harris (1964–1995), former colonel of Moore Town and a Jamaican government legislative member, cites the Asante as the Maroons' main origin. "The majority of Maroons, as my ancestors came to be referred to, originally came from West Africa. Through oral tradition, claims are made that the majority of those who came were mainly of the Ashanti ethnic group, who were forcibly brought to Jamaica as slaves by the Spaniards."[31] What is important to note is not the veracity of the claim, since some of such claims cannot be substantiated, but the claim itself.

Basically, the claims to African origin in the oral histories made by Maroons have critical implications. They are ideological arguments for recognition as human civilized subjects. They are claims of having a long history and connection to ancient cultures and civilizations in Africa as a whole, and at other times to specific African peoples.

Traditions

The Maroons make phenomenological claims of origin not only in oral history but in traditional practices that include tangible and intangible cultural expressions. We can say that Maroon traditions are multifarious, where the notion of tradition refers to enduring cultural patterns that evoke continuity with the past. In Maroon communities, tradition is both the experience of actual continuity and the belief that certain practices are legitimate because of their antiquity. In these respects, Maroon traditions, like those of the wider Jamaican population, are in many instances hybridized, with African, European, and Amerindian influences.

The traditions of Maroon communities are impacted by the geographic locations of their often-dispersed members. Many Maroons live outside their designated territory in Jamaica. Hence, probably the majority of Maroons interact and live with people who may not share the same traditions or culture, and some Maroons are perceived like, or actually behave no differently culturally from, other Jamaicans in their traditional practices. Also, the inclusive nature of the formation of Maroon community, which is based on lineage, makes it possible for any persons, regardless of their cultural background, to be considered Maroon, as long as they can trace their ancestry to any of the original communities. This allows members who may have been completely culturally detached from self-identified Maroon populations for years or even generations to become part of the community, thus creating a people who have complex cultural traditions and practices.

Although they draw on several traditions, Maroons claim African traditions as the most important. For this reason, the focus in this section is on these claimed African traditions and their significance. However, the writing is not intended to argue the veracity of "tradition" or a claimed tradition of being "African" or not, but rather, to explore how it is understood as African by the Maroons. In this respect, the book examines the rhetorical strategies as they pertain to claims about traditions in order to explore the interpretation of Maroons in the matter. In other words, I examine how Maroons express and represent their traditions and provide meaning to them by examining the hermeneutics and semiotics of their texts, oral histories, performances and rituals, artifacts, etc., and what they signify.

Maroons readily articulate the significance of what they consider their treasured African traditions, and many Maroon leaders and elders have been troubled by the dilution of the African beliefs and practices in their communities. As early as the 1960s, former Colonel C. L. G. Harris (1964–1995) of Moore Town stated with concern that Maroons have "maintained certain traditions" but "some of these more important customs have been passing away."[32] In an interview in 2012, Colonel Ferron Williams (2009–present) of Accompong Town observed that he would "love" to see the maintenance of their fading "African tradition" in every way, including in "words, food, and dress."[33] In early 2013, Garfield Rowe, Accompong Town council member and principal of the local school, stated that "if we are not careful, we are going to lose a lot of our culture, a lot of our history, and a lot of our tradition."[34] He had observed that the "younger folks tend to want to adopt more to the American and European sort of cultures instead of the African."[35] Internal community dialogue on the preservation of African traditional (indigenous) practice is common. The point here of referring to Maroons' fear of cultural erosion is to highlight the significance they place on African cultural traditions and their desire to maintain them. It is a critical practice that challenges the Westernization and abjection of their cultural forms.

Intangible Cultural Forms

Claims related to cultural forms are critical in the Maroons' enunciation of links with Africa. Bilby argues that the culture of the Maroons "came to reside almost entirely in intangibles such as values, ethics, and consciousness of a shared past—as well as coded forms of expressive culture."[36] Indeed, the symbolic practice of Maroons' cultural traditions associated with Africa is most evident in political and land-tenure systems, language, belief systems, and the arts.

In political terms, all Maroon communities consider a traditional (indigenous) African system as the foundation of their current governing and land-tenure systems. Maroons argue that they have maintained their African political system for more than 300 years. Furthermore, they specifically lay claim to the Akan political system in the founding of their communities.[37] Here origin is linked to the socio-political organization of the communities (this will be further explored in chapter five).

Language, too, is used as a signifier of African practice and a critical practice of Maroons in resisting Western hegemony by attempting to maintain the language. The Maroons speak English, Jamaican Patois, and Kromanti. The Kromanti language—or rather, dialect—of the Maroons is an important symbolic link to Africa. In the academic literature, it is well established that Kromanti has been strongly influenced by the Twi language of the Akan people in West Africa, and thus is a concrete link to the African continent, particularly Ghana. Kromanti is reflected in the Maroons' lexicon with such words as *Abeng*, *asafo*, and *sankofa*, and cultural practices including the Kromanti Play, storytelling, and Kromanti songs, as we will explore.

In the early part of the twentieth century, the anthropologist Joseph Williams, viewing the Kromanti language as highly influenced by Twi, found it to be in varying states of decline. In Accompong Town, he found the decline to be most evident, but the language to be spoken and in better condition among the elders in Moore Town. In Charles Town and Scot's Hall, the language was in the best shape, with children being taught it.[38] Colonel Williams (2009–present) stated that in Moore Town the name for Maroons was "Brewfro Ashanti." meaning "Once were Ashanti," referring to efforts to preserve tradition and maintain African-derived practices. [39]

In the second half of the twentieth century, other scholars acknowledged Kromanti's influence and explored the language in greater detail. According to Carey, Dr. Joe Adamofio, a Ghanaian who visited Moore Town in 1959, thought that the Maroons were speaking Twi.[40] The linguists Mervyn Alleyne and Bev Hall-Alleyne concluded that Twi dominates the Kromanti language.[41] The anthropologist Kenneth Bilby and linguist David Dalby support the idea that Kromanti is similar to Twi with a smattering of other influences.[42] At the same time, Alleyne and Dalby maintain that Kromanti is not a fully functional language but, rather, an "esoteric repository of isolated words and sets of phrases."[43]

Today, in Accompong Town, some Maroons know a few words and phrases of Kromanti, but any more seems to be only a memory. According to Deputy Colonel Melville Currie of Accompong Town, a few people spoke Kromanti, apparently in his parents' generation, during healing ceremonies and Kromanti songs.[44] The Maroon elder James Chambers of Accompong Town states that many older people knew the language, but they passed away without having taught it to the younger people. He mentioned the influential elder Nanny Rowe as one of the speakers who recently passed away.[45] Rowe's grandson Lance Ricketts said he learned a few words from his grandmother.[46] He mentioned words such as *binequa* as meaning "non-Maroon," *Obruni* for "white man," and *Nyankipong* meaning "God."[47] Although the language has faded, the Maroons use the remaining lexicon to emphasize their African origin.

In the Windward Maroon communities of Charles Town, Moore Town, and Scot's Hall, there is a wider range and use of Kromanti words and phrases. As the Maroon descendant of Moore Town Bev Carey remarks, "The Maroons spoke several languages. However, the most common was one which the Maroons called Kromanti, closely resembling the African form of the Twi tongue."[48] Former Colonel Harris (1964–1995) of Moore Town also traces the Maroon language of the Kromanti to the Twi language spoken by the Asante people.[49] He readily cites a range of Kromanti words that he deems to be from the Akan language. For instance, he says that the name of God as *Nyamkopong* or *Nyame* and certain objects and items such as *unsu* [Twi: *nsuo*] (water), *edwiani* [Twi: *aduane*] (food), *kwedu* [Twi: *kwadu*] (banana), *ekutu* [Twi: *akutuo*] (orange), and *prako* (pig) indicate the Maroons' West African connections and Akan origin.[50]

Maroon leaders such as Colonels Lumsden (2004–2015), Prehay (c. 1983–2016), and Sterling (1995–present) often greet each other and other people in Kromanti. At the Quao Day celebration in Charles Town in 2012, the then-Colonel Prehay (c. 1983–2016) of Scot's Hall taught the audience that *nso* means "water," *nsa* is "rum," and *enpaypay* means "knife."[51] In any case, this residual lexicon is used as a signifier of African roots.

For the Maroons, the connection of Kromanti to Africa is significant for a number of reasons. Kromanti words are used to bring to light the African connections that are linked to the communities' survival. Maroons celebrate their language as a critical practice and their ability to preserve their African history and tradition despite British colonialism and slavery. Kromanti is conjured up to increase the spiritual, cultural, and social significance of events, be they public gatherings, healing ceremonies, or pouring libations. It is also used ritualistically (see chapter four for more details). More than that of any other group of African descent in the West Indies, the Maroons' ability to maintain an African tradition in language is viewed as the reason they successfully established and have maintained sovereign communities. Fundamentally, Kromanti is used as a way to enunciate African origin.

As for belief systems, there are different religious practices that overlap in forms and are enunciated as African practices in the Maroon communities. Although Christianity is officially and formally practiced, Maroons make references to African-derived belief systems in the rituals that relate to their everyday life.[52] The main African-derived belief systems are Kromanti Play, Obeah, and Myal.[53] The syncretized Christianity of the Maroon may or may not be considered by some Maroons as African, but Kromanti Play, Obeah, and Myal certainly are. Maroon individuals may practice all three plus Christianity, or just one if they prefer one belief system over the others. This section will focus on the three spiritual systems through which Maroons make firm rhetorical and symbolic claims of being of African origin.

A significant traditional belief system in Maroon communities claimed to be African is Obeah, or Science. The Maroons believe that their practice of Obeah originated in Africa. Asked for specifics, most Maroons point to its source as being Kromanti or from present-day Ghana. In the *Encyclopedia of Jamaican Heritage*, Olive Senior argues that the root of the practice is in West Africa, and the origin of the word may be *bayi* or *obayifo* from Akan.[54] In contrast, Kwasi Konadu, in *The Akan Diaspora in the Americas*, mentions recent dissent about the Akan origin of the word and argues that *dibia* in Igbo is a more likely source.[55] Maroons themselves contend that Akan, Igbo, and other African groups all influenced the development of Obeah. The bottom line is that the Maroons claim the origin of the practice to be in Africa, giving it great symbolic significance.

In ideological terms, many Maroons see Obeah as spiritually momentous and powerfully significant, given its African origin. They believe that they were able to overcome the British because their powers were derived from continuing African traditional (indigenous) practices. Hence, there is a politics of representation at play here in the different narrations of Obeah, tying in directly to Diaspora as a critical practice that challenges black abjection.

Harris Cawley, pastor of the United Church of Accompong Town and a former colonel (1984–1988), describes the belief system and its history in the Accompong community as follows:

> It is something that has come from Africa with the Africans. It was with them. It is practiced even in my day. In the early 1940s, there were men who practiced Obeah. Obeah was something that was against the government of the day. But the Maroons have an exclusive state, so they were allowed to do what they want. So people generally come out here and ride up into Accompong, accessibly up the road. So there were quite a few Obeah men because they made money. So it was the occupation. People would come from, even from Kingston, and prominent men, too. And these men who were the Obeah men, they had a family, they lived in a house, and since they were making money, they lived a kind of lavish life, above the ordinary man.[56]

What is important here is that the Maroons believe that Obeah came from Africa. Perhaps what is most significant is that it directly challenges notions of modernity by claiming that its practitioners are modern, in material terms, and that it was a service provided to "modern" people.

In the context of claiming an African worldview, former Colonel Cawley elaborates on how an Obeah man and woman engage their spirits:

> Every man has a spirit. You have a spirit; I have a spirit. Okay, the spirit that is within us is alive that we get from the Creator, that is in us. So sometimes when a man dies, his body is going to raise and interact or interfere with people. So they [Obeah persons] always want to trap that spirit, so that they can put that spirit into subjection to their will. That is where the Obeah and the spirit come in. But not everyone is the person who is a wicked man. It is easier for them to interact. But if he was a righteous man, it is hard for them to break that. So if the man was righteous and godly, and feared god, it would be hard for that Obeah man to get that spirit to do his will. But when the man is not righteous and loves a wicked life, they can get him to do wicked acts. That is how I understand it, because they used to work and they say that these things work.[57]

This is a reference to the universality of the spirit as a foundation for all humanity, locating African practice in the domain of universal humanity, and rejecting colonial exclusion as being of bad faith.

The practitioners who work with the spirits of the dead tend to consider themselves scientists who are continuing African spiritual practices. James Chambers, a self-acknowledged practitioner of Science, believes that the practitioners' powers come from Africa. He states that all of the early Maroon leaders such as Kojo, Nanny, and Accompong, who were Africans, "were high in the Science."[58] He believes that many people outside of Accompong Town are afraid of the Maroons because of their powerful African-derived Science.[59]

Another related belief system of the Maroons is Myal, which is also claimed to be African in origin (although that is disputed by scholars such as Jean Besson). The Maroons see Myal as a system of communicating with the ancestors, usually through spiritual possession.[60] According to former Colonel Cawley, "Myalism is a mysterious operation of an individual under spiritualistic influence."[61] It is a belief system not only of the Maroons but practiced by the wider Jamaican society. Senior describes Myal as "an old religion concerned with healing in Jamaica."[62]

Many Maroons see Myal as being an African tradition that values the powers and influence of their ancestors. In this cosmology, the most powerful of the ancestors are those who were born in Africa. As Carey describes:

> Maroons believed that their ancestors were wiser and greater than they themselves; that these ancestral spirits were around them or within call; that they cast a watchful eye over events in the community, shared its concerns; that these ancestral spirits often frowned on the action of their offspring but could also be pleased. They felt that these ancestors could reach out to them and give them their wisdom, and, indeed, they actively sought out these relationships between the other [spiritual] world and the real world in which they lived.[63]

The claim here is to being African through the ancestors. Former Colonel Harris Cawley (1984–1988) of Accompong Town observes that Myal did originate with their ancestors in Africa.[64] According to Hansley Reid, the Abeng Blower of Accompong Town (Abeng is a type of horn), if the "necromantic spirits" should come into someone, the ancestors such as Kojo, Nanny, or Dundi may come through that individual.[65] Colonel Williams (2009–present), speaking on behalf of the Accompong's cultural dancers, believes that many of the dancers experience ancestral possession and he states that when persons are in Myal, "they do not know what they are doing and what has taken place until they get out of Myal."[66]

In Accompong Town, Myal experience is most evident in the annual Kojo Day celebration. Former Colonel Cawley sees Myal as a way to exhibit the goodwill of the ancestors, influencing the community positively.[67] Often, the cultural dancers of Accompong Town are spiritually possessed and say that they are talking to the ancestors. It is a time of drumming, singing, and dancing, with the pouring of libations, similar to practices today among some of the Akans of Ghana.

Kromanti Play, which overlaps and is interconnected with Obeah, is also claimed to have roots in Africa. Some Maroons use these terms interchangeably to refer to the same belief system. It is in the Windward Maroon communities, particularly of Moore Town, that the highly secretive and infrequent Kromanti Play is most readily identified and prevalent. According to former Colonel Harris (1964–1995) of Moore Town:

> Through the years, the Maroons maintained certain traditions and rituals which not only kept them a closely knit organization but evoked the wonder, admiration, and respect of others. . . . Then, too, was the continual drumming and dancing—spoken of at [Kromanti] "Play"—which is credited with cures bordering on the miraculous. This particular operation is not easy to describe—one must see it to understand—and yet such a statement may be woefully misleading, since being a witness, especially an alien one, could indeed make understanding more difficult. The "dancerman" was one of a special set who entered the "ring" (a circular opening formed by the drummers, ordinary dancers, singers, and spectators) when the singing and drumming reached a crescendo and the dancing its peak of eeriness. Every action of his—even his speech—was changed to that of the particular departed kin whose spirit had now found habitation in his body. In this state, he revealed the past and unfolded the future with mystifying accuracy: explicit instructions were given on any special subject under consideration. After this someone skilled in the art sent the spirit back on its way, and the dancer man once more became a normal person. He was then said to be "cleared."[68]

Former Colonel Harris traces the origin of this practice to Africa, particularly to the Akans. This passage relates to the direct claim to Africa and African wisdom through ancestor possession. Even further, its significance is not merely to locate Africa within the domain of a universal humanity; it is also a critical practice that challenges European claims to superiority by positing African culture and the central role that spirituality plays as an essential human trait (a view of spirituality that is rejected by Europe, or more precisely, what Europe is represented to be in the modern era).

In 2012, the then Colonel Noel Prehay (c. 1983–2016) of Scot's Hall stated that Kromanti Play is from Africa. He mentioned it as a practice shared only among the Windward Maroons of Scot's Hall, Charles Town, and Moore Town.[69] He described it as drumming and dancing generally intended to heal the sick, cure disease, and ward off evil occurrences.[70]

Obeah, Myal, and Kromanti Play, all claimed to be African, are interrelated concepts and practices. Maroons originally used the term "Obeah" to refer to ancestral powers associated with Kromanti Play, but many Maroons prefer the term "Science," because Obeah has been stigmatized.[71] Senior understands that the colonial authorities and the literature on the matter have conflated elements of what she calls the "African religious complex" that were brought to the Caribbean, whether by medicine men, priests, or other practitioners.[72] She argues that it was Europeans who designated all the spiritual belief systems as Obeah. In a *Businessweek* article in 2012, the then Colonel Prehay (c. 1983–2016) of Scot's Hall said that "Our Obeah is a good Obeah."[73] He was presumably referring not to only Obeah per se, but Myal and Kromanti Play as well. Arguably, the point is that the practices are conflated from several original ones, the specific attributions of the Maroon's religions in present-day representation notwithstanding.

Many Maroons, Jamaicans, and scholars believe that Maroons practice an especially potent form of these African-derived belief systems. Although Obeah and Myal are shared with other African descendants, Maroons are viewed as having a stronger expression of the practices, and Kromanti Play is unique to the Maroons. Many Maroons argue that their ability to harness supernatural powers to achieve protection and destroy their enemies is based on their preserved African spiritual belief systems. It is the belief, which continues in Jamaica today, that the spiritual world can impact the physical world that made the Maroon communities viable and a sovereign space during British colonial rule.

Another claimed signification of African tradition besides language and beliefs is the arts, the forms of which are interconnected with other claimed African traditions. In the Maroon communities, specific art forms are celebrated and linked to African traditions: literary, visual, and performance arts.

As a literary art form, storytelling in Maroon communities is symbolically linked to an African past and readily acknowledged as historically significant. According to the Moore Town writer McFarlane, Kojo "was a spellbinding speaker who could hold with equal ease the attention of the mountain village Maroons or that of his regular soldiers with tales and 'Anancy' [Ananse] stories."[74] Further, as Maroon author Carey testifies, "Evenings found the children gathered by the older folk, where they were regaled with stories from the African homeland, of the prankster Anancy, and of the wild animals and beasts which they would never see, except in their imagination."[75] Although Ananse stories can be heard throughout the West Indies, they are nevertheless significant in Maroon identity as a means of connecting to Africa.[76]

Indeed, storytelling links to Africa, especially Ananse stories, have a long history in Maroon communities. Their significance and popularity have been referenced by many observers over the years, including Katherine Dunham in the 1930s.[77] In the 1960s, the popularity of the Ananse stories was even covered in the African American newspaper *Afro-American*, highlighting their link to Ghanaian folklore.[78] In the 1970s, Laura Tanna collected some African-derived folklore in Jamaica, including a few Ananse stories in Accompong Town.[79]

The Maroons try to keep the African-linked art form of storytelling alive, deeming it an important symbolic link to African tradition in their everyday lives. Today, many of the Maroon communities' elders can recite a number of stories, particularly Ananse stories, that are linked directly to the Akan peoples of today. In both Accra and Cape Coast in Ghana, the author conversed with many Akan individuals who could tell Ananse stories similar to those of the Maroon communities.

Besides storytelling, another significant art form is ceremonial/ritual performance, which holds great symbolic significance as an indicator of African practice. Ceremonial performance usually comes in the form of singing, drumming, and dancing. The Maroons see it as a continuation of African traditions, especially as it is shared by many other peoples of African descent. At just about every community or public event, including conferences, burials, marching, and the annual Independence Day celebrations, the Maroons sing, drum, and dance.[80] The ceremonial rituals are also linked with the Maroons' belief systems (Myal, Obeah, and Kromanti Play), political system, and language.

The Maroons themselves trace their rituals to Africa. According to Reid, the music and dance of the Maroons come from Africa:

> Cudjoe [Kojo], Nanny, and Dundi learned that their people were being captured as slaves on the ships, so they joined them on the slave ship with their four-corner [Gumbé] drums, their shakers, and their square drum and came to Jamaica at Morant Point in St. Thomas in the east. They worked with the slave masters there for about 3 to 4 days, then they started to play the drums and the shakers and dance and sing their Kromanti, and there came the evil spirit from the Kromanti song, which dealt with them [the English]. When the slaves heard the Kromanti from where they were, they knew that it was their people, so they traced them and then they had a rebellion against the English. They started the rebellion in the east and ended it in the west. When Cudjoe [Kojo] and Nanny started the war and got all their people, they began to slay the butcher's pigs and eat them. They ripped all the food from the vineyard and they [the Maroons] ate and drank it.[81]

This is an etiology of African origin upon which claims to an African present are based.

The Maroons' songs are claimed to originate in Africa. As Carey asserts, Maroons' "songs were woven into their stories of long past Africa, of the experiences and victories of their ancestors."[82] Former Colonel Martin-Luther Wright (1967–1984 and 1988–1993) of Accompong Town reported to the musicologist Jacqueline Cogdell DjeDje saying that the language of many of the songs are mixed. He said in the old days, Accompong Maroons sang their songs in an African language but they do not do it anymore. But he said if you go over to Moore Town and Scot's Hall, there the African language is fluently spoken.[83]

The Kromanti songs in and of themselves might not be about Africa or necessarily identical to any specific African tradition of music, but their roots are viewed as being based in Africa by the Maroons. Lance Ricketts, a farmer and tour guide from Accompong, does consider Kromanti songs to be African songs.[84] Although the songs are significantly creolized, many Maroons insist that the Kromanti songs continue their African tradition.

As DjeDje observes, the Kromanti songs are a fusion of elements from various African and European cultures in form, melody, and rhythmic organization. She notes that the African component is similar "to a West African drum ensemble, where the master drummer is the primary improviser; the vocal leader in a Maroon ensemble can be regarded as the 'master' musician, because she freely and spontaneously changes her part."[85] DjeDje also noticed that, as in many African musical traditions, call-and-response was central to the performance, and the melodies of the songs performed are based on additive rhythms, a hallmark of African music.[86]

In Accompong Town, those Kromanti songs that are considered to be more influenced by Africa are associated with burials in the community. In the 1930s, Dunham witnessed Kromanti grave-digging songs.[87] Bilby observed that it is customary for Maroon grave-diggers to stop working at some point to pour libations over the site and sing a number of Kromanti songs.[88] In interviews, Accompong Maroons said they identify grave-digging songs as significantly African. The Maroon elder James Chambers of Accompong Town identifies many such songs as some of the most African in form.[89]

The eastern Maroons also sing Kromanti songs, sometimes similar to those of the Accompong Maroons and sometimes different. Former Colonel C. L. G. Harris (1964–1995) of Moore Town avers that the songs sung during Kromanti Play are "categorised as Coromante, Sa Leone, Pappa, and Jawbone. The first lends itself to fierce dancing; the next two are of a slow galloping rhythm and are sung mostly when it is pleasure time; the last named is sad and soul-stirring."[90] The "heavier" categories of songs are named after a number of "tribes" or "nations" that are said to have contributed to early Maroon society and refer to certain regions or peoples in Africa.[91]

Overall, the arts, especially storytelling and music, are deployed to signify African origin. They speak to a claimed African past, and some of them are positioned and believed to be shared with many groups of Africans, especially the Akan peoples. These practices serve as enunciations of African origin that are critical in the articulation of Diaspora.

Tangible Cultural Forms

To bolster Maroons' arguments, certain tangible cultural forms are also used to link the communities to Africa. It is important to examine the signifying objects of material culture, which differ across the various Jamaican Maroon communities, and how they are used in claims of African authenticity and origin. Some are specific to particular communities, while others are shared by different communities. The most popular of these objects are musical instruments.

The Abeng is the most ubiquitous and celebrated of the objects used to signify African origin in Jamaican Maroon communities. Its name comes from the Twi word Abɛn, and it originated in what is now Ghana. The instrument is made from a cow's horn, similar to the way it is made in Ghana.[92]

The history of the Abeng has been traced to the Maroons' emergence in the seventeenth and eighteenth centuries, and since then has played a central role in the narrating of Maroon history and culture.[93] Among the islands of the Caribbean, it is unique to Jamaican Maroons.[94] Maroons consider the Abeng as occupying a central role in their communities' founding and subsequent development. Its use has even been institutionalized by the incorporation of an Abeng Blower as an official in the governing Maroon Council.

In 2011, the Chief Abeng Blower of Accompong, Hansley Reid, explained the origin and other significance of the instrument in the following way:

> The Maroons carried four Abengs from Africa to Jamaica, and there were four men who were in charge of blowing the Abeng, which was the only source of communication in Jamaica for the Maroons at the time. One was in Stone Gutter Spanish Town, St. Jago de la Vega, the other was in Manchester at Williamsfield, [an]other was in Balaclava, and one on top of the Peace Cave as a community blower to tell the people how far away the enemy was from them. So the person from Spanish Town would send the echo, telling them that the enemy is coming and how far away they are, the person from Williamsfield would receive that echo, then send it to the person in Balaclava, then the one in Trelawny Town Accompong picked it up and sent it out. Then it was scattered all around, so they could know how to ambush the British.[95]

The Abeng, considered one of the few physical objects that came over from Africa, is important for several reasons. Originally, it was useful for the protection and preservation of Maroon culture against the British colonialists. Its long and ancient use in Africa and the Caribbean makes it also an important symbol of Maroon independence. It appears on the national flag of the Accompong Maroons. It is also an instrument used to play the unique African-derived Kromanti music of the Maroons. According to Reid, the Abeng is still blown to acknowledge special occasions such as community gatherings and the passing away of community members, and for the annual Maroon Independence Day celebration. Furthermore, the Maroons use the Abeng to facilitate communication with their ancestors, as do the Akan people to which it is linked.[96] The author witnessed this at the Asante Akwasiade Festival on June 22, 2014, in Kumasi, Ghana.

Other popular and notable instruments in Jamaican Maroon communities are drums, especially the Gumbé, which is linked to African traditional (indigenous) practices. Drums have become a universal symbol in the making of claims of African origin by other communities of African descent throughout the world. Maroons view the drum as a specifically African musical instrument. When Maroons identify a specific place for the drum's origin, they often refer to the present-day country of Ghana. In Accompong Town, many Maroons claim that the Gumbé drum came from the Asante and Kromanti (Akan) in Ghana.

There are different views on the naming of the Gumbé. Dalby believes that the word is derived from the Bantu word *Ngoma*, a generic term for drum in central, eastern, and southern Africa.[97] Further narrowing down the origin of the word, the historian Kwasi Konadu contends that the drum's name stems from the Bakongo people.[98]

Senior cites the use of the Gumbé drum in different parts of Jamaica as well as in the rest of the Caribbean and West Africa.[99] The anthropologist Werner Zips in his research found the Gumbé to be similar to the drum used on special occasions among the present-day Ga and Fante peoples of Ghana.[100] In my research in Ghana, I did not observe the use of any similar drums to the Gumbé by the Asante or Fante, although the Gome, a square drum played with both hands and feet, was found in ceremonial use by the Ga people in Accra.

The scholar Rachel Jackson, in "The Trans-Atlantic Journey of Gumbé," traces the origin of the Gumbé drum among the Jamaican Maroons, arguing that it was modeled on various pre-slavery African drums. She further postulates that the Maroons of Cudjoe Town, who were deported to Nova Scotia, then Sierra Leone, introduced the drum to the African continent in the nineteenth century, then it spread to about a dozen West and Central African countries, making a trans-Atlantic loop.[101] In Ghana, it is believed that Gold Coast migrants got it from Sierra Leoneans, then it became indigenized by the Ga people in the form of the Gome drum.[102]

The drum is used as a signifying practice of African origin in many ways. It is played in the Maroons' unique Kromanti music. It takes part in the African diasporic religious expressions, such as Kromanti Play, being important in summoning the most powerful of the African-born ancestors. Overall, the drum is valued as a traditional instrument that came from Africa. Once again, its significance is the role it plays in the assertions of African authenticity, whether or not it can or could be found in a specific place in Africa.

Windward Maroons have some other instruments that are considered African, including the *oprenteng* drum, *kwat* (made from bamboo), and *adawo* (a machete struck with a piece of metal).[103]

As Deputy Colonel Melville Currie of Accompong indicates, a few jewelry items are deemed African. Some of these items to be worn come from trees, such as what they call the *kakoon* and the *nikala*, or *walli*. Currie and other community members assert they are used in Africa.[104]

On ceremonial occasions, a few objects are displayed to showcase African connections. For example, Maroon leaders and cultural performers often wear traditional African garments at public gatherings. As a case in point, a full-page spread of Maroon elders dressed in "traditional African gear" was displayed in the *Jamaica Gleaner* on January 8, 2009.[105]

One can see signifying elements of African connections in architecture and community artwork. Yet many Maroons believe that African architecture used to be much more popular in the communities, mainly in the building of thatched roof houses.[106] In contemporary times, Maroons identify a few structures that they claim are directly linked to Africa. In Charles Town, there is an Asafo Yard Complex that has a stage, a courtyard, and a museum. The idea of an *Asafo* comes from the same word in Akan that has been used in Charles Town and neighboring Moore Town communities to refer to a meeting place, usually of warriors. The term, therefore, references traditional (indigenous) African practice and form.

In addition to the architectural complex, there are a few murals and works of art related to Africa in Charles Town. One wall of the Asafo Yard Complex tells the story of the Maroons' origin in Africa as "kings and queens," their journey through the Middle Passage, and their struggles in Jamaica. A sankofa bird is carved into the door of the museum.[107] *Sankofa* (Twi: *sankɔfa*) is an Akan word meaning to "reach back and get it."[108] I have observed these images in several Ghanaian cities and towns, such as Kumasi, Accra, and Elmina. As the *Jamaica Gleaner* mentions, for former Colonel Lumsden (2004–2015) of Charles Town, the images epitomize the preservation of Maroon history and heritage through art: African forms inscribed in Maroon identity.[109]

The point here is that the claim to African authenticity relates to the contemporary presence of the practices and forms we have just discussed. The particular question here relates to how those claims are enunciated and what they signify. What is unique and special about the Maroons is that their claims are to a much "purer" form of African culture and practice than that found in Jamaica and the wider Americas.

Of the four Maroon communities, Accompong Town has the greatest number of historical and cultural sites linked to Africa, including the African burial grounds, Sealed Grounds, Kindah Tree, and Herbal Garden. They are sites symbolic of African connections and uniqueness.

There are two main sites for African burial grounds. The first is located in northeast Accompong Town: the Asante, Kromanti, and Kongo burial ground. The Maroons claim it as living testimony of the African origin of their people. Also, Old Accompong Town is where Kojo and other ancient Maroon leaders are buried.[110]

There are sixty Sealed Grounds throughout Accompong Town that are considered by the Maroons to be African. These special sites are supernatural areas where various ceremonies are held to protect and celebrate the community, also signifying African authenticity. In many respects, the sites are more than a belief and are inscribed in the Maroon' ways of being and consciousness of self. The important issue is their signifying import, or semiotics. They are meanings embedded in symbolic communication and symbolic interaction. They are sites to connect with the ancestral spirits, associated with the belief system of Myal.[111] They stem from claimed African forms of religious and spiritual practice imbued with symbolic significance in Maroon practice.

The Kindah Tree, an ancient mango tree, represents African unity for the Maroons.[112] It was where the different groups of Africans—especially the Asante, Kromanti, and Kongo—came together in a blood pact to unite to fight the British. For the Accompong Maroons, the Kindah Tree represents the unity of different groups of Africans.

The other site of symbolic maintenance of African traditions is the Herbal Garden. By 2018, it was in disrepair, although in the past it symbolized the importance of herbal lore tied to African origin. The Garden was an offshoot of the work done by the Accompong Traditional Medicinal Creative Group and Youth Project in the 1990s. The group's stated objective was to serve "as an educational vehicle to teach plant identification and management, reforestation, processing, and ecology."[113] Lawrence Rowe worked with the youth group. He and others refer to the physical structure in the garden as the "Asante Hut." Its circular shape and thatched roof are reminiscent of West African huts. He continues to believe that the hut's use is to preserve and conserve medicinal herbs that continue a claimed African way of life.[114] It represents more the continuity of African traditional (indigenous) practice than the goal of preservation and conservation.

The namings of some of the Maroon communities are considered to be African. The main Leeward Maroon community that was destroyed in the late eighteenth century was originally called Cudjoe Town. Cudjoe is the anglicized Akan name of Kwadwo or Kojo. Additionally, the name of Accompong is claimed to be a derivation of the popular Akan name of Akyeampong (anglicized Acheampong).[115]

In all of these practices and sites, one can see the symbolic significance of tangible cultural forms in claims about African origin, related to the production and reproduction of the "African-ness" of Maroon identity. Such significance is linked to the understanding that "African" culture has allowed the Maroons to substantiate the claims of an authentic African presence.

Conclusion

Maroons enunciate and make linkages to peoples of Africa through their claims to origin in Africa. Maroons' claims to African origin are in their oral histories. They are in their Kromanti language. They are in their political, land tenure, and spiritual systems. They are in their storytelling, songs, and ceremonial/ritual performances. They are in the very name of the communities of Accompong Town (derived from Akyeampong in Twi) and Cudjoe Town (derived from Kojo and Kwadwo). They are in the community's sacred sites of Kindah, the Sealed Grounds, and the African burial grounds. They are in their use of objects, such as the Abeng. They are in the naming of structures, such as the Asafo Yard and the Asante Hut.

Beyond whether multiple sources and perspectives agree that Maroons are from Africa, the meaning and significance Maroons' attribute to these links are what is important. It is a critical practice and ideological struggle, challenging European racist thought about black abjection. Resistance to black abjection and claims of origin are two of the central bases in the development of collective consciousness.

Notes

1. Wallace Sterling, interview by author, Moore Town, Portland, Jamaica, December 1, 2011.

2. Parts of this chapter were previously published in *Symbolism* and used with permission. Mario Nisbett, "African Diasporic Traditional Symbols and Claims," in *Rüdiger Ahrens*, *Florian Kläger*, Keith A. Sandiford and Klaus Stierstorfer (eds.) of *Symbolism: An International Annual of Critical Aesthetics*, Volume 16, Berlin, Germany: De Gruyter, 2016, pp. 117–138. Mario Nisbett, "Claiming Asante: The Akan Origins of Jamaican Maroons," in *The Asante World (17–21st Century)*, eds. Edmund Abaka and Kwame Osei Kwarteng (New York: Routledge, 2021), 255–277.

3. Paul Gilroy, *The Black Atlantic: Modernity and Double Consciousness* (Cambridge, Mass.: Harvard University Press, 1993), 112.

4. Stuart Hall, "Cultural Identity and Diaspora," in *Identity: Community, Culture, Difference*, ed. Jonathan Rutherford (London: Lawrence & Wishart, 1990), 224–25; Stuart Hall, "Thinking the Diaspora: Home-Thoughts from Abroad," *Small Axe: A Journal of Criticism* no. 6 (1999): 13.

5. Stuart Hall, "The Problem of Ideology: Marxism without Guarantees," in *Stuart Hall: Critical Dialogues in Cultural Studies,* eds. David Morley and Kuan-Hsing Chen (New York: Taylor & Francis, 1996), 36.

6. Jorge Larrain, "Stuart Hall and the Marxist Concept of Ideology," in *Stuart Hall: Critical Dialogues in Cultural Studies,* eds. David Morley and Kuan-Hsing Chen (New York: Taylor & Francis, 1996), 47.

7. The present-day Maroons of Jamaica all believe they were descended from "Spanish Maroons" before they divided into the Windward and Leeward groups and then into the four current communities (Accompong Town, Charles Town, Moore Town, and Scot's Hall).

8. H. A. Rowe, "The Maroon's Celebration," *Jamaica Gleaner* (Kingston), March 22, 1938.

9. Colonel Martin-Luther Wright, "Accompong Maroons of Jamaica," in *Maroon Heritage Archaeological, Ethnographic, and Historical Perspectives,* ed. E. Kofi Agorsah (Barbados: Canoe Press, 1994), 64.

10. Ibid., 67.

11. Harris Cawley, interview by author, Accompong Town, St. Elizabeth, Jamaica, August 01, 2012.

12. Ibid.

13. Melville Currie, interview by author, Accompong Town, St. Elizabeth, Jamaica, August 14, 2012.

14. Lawrence Rowe and Lance Ricketts, interview by author, Accompong Town, St. Elizabeth, Jamaica, January 8, 2012.

15. Ibid.

16. Ibid.

17. Ibid.

18. Ibid.

19. Milton C. McFarlane, *Cudjoe of Jamaica: Pioneer for Black Freedom in the New World* (Short Hills, NJ: R. Enslow, 1977), 18, 24.

20. Ibid., 18.

21. Kwasi Konadu, *The Akan Diaspora in the Americas* (New York: Oxford University Press, 2010), 122–123.

22. McFarlane, *Cudjoe of Jamaica*, 40.

23. Ibid., 126.

24. Sterling, interview.

25. Ibid.

26. "Uncovered: Nanny of the Maroons," *Flair Magazine*, October 20, 2003, 5.

27. Bev Carey, *The Maroon Story: The Authentic and Original History of the Maroons in the History of Jamaica, 1490–1880* (Gordon Town, Jamaica: Agouti Press, 1997), 1, 175–76.

28. Ibid., 185.

29. Ibid., 406.

30. Ibid., 185 and 426.

31. C. L. G. Harris, "The True Traditions of my Ancestors," in *Maroon Heritage: Archaeological, Ethnographic, and Historical Perspectives*, ed. E. Kofi Agorsah (Barbados: Canoe Press, 1994), 36.

32. C. L. G. Harris, "The Spirit of Nanny," *Jamaica Gleaner* (Kingston), August 6, 1967.

33. Ferron Williams, interview by author, Accompong Town, St. Elizabeth, Jamaica, January 7, 2012.

34. Garfield Rowe, interview by author, Accompong Town, St. Elizabeth, Jamaica, January 10, 2013.

35. Ibid.

36. Kenneth Bilby, *True-Born Maroon* (Gainsville, University Press of Florida, 2005) 30.

37. Michael A. Gomez, *Exchanging Our Country Marks: The Transformation of African Identities in the Colonial and Antebellum South* (Chapel Hill: The University of North Carolina Press, 1998), 109.

38. Mervyn C. Alleyne and Bev Hall-Alleyne, "Language Maintenance and Language Death in the Caribbean," *Caribbean Quarterly* 28, no. 4 (1982): 57; Joseph Williams, *The Maroons of Jamaica* (Chestnut Hill, Mass.: Boston College Press, 1938), 464.

39. "Fr. J. Williams and the Life of the Maroons," *Jamaica Gleaner* (Kingston), July 12, 1937; Williams, *Maroons of Jamaica*, 465.

40. Carey, *Maroon Story*, 185.

41. Mervyn C. Alleyne and Bev Hall-Alleyne, "Language Maintenance and Language Death in the Caribbean," *Caribbean Quarterly* 28, no. 4 (1982): 55.

42. Kenneth Bilby, "The Kromanti Dance of the Windward Maroons of Jamaica," *New West Indian Guide* 55, no. 1 (1981): 65; David Dalby, "Ashanti Survivals in the Language and Traditions of the Windward Maroons of Jamaica," *African Language Studies no.* 12 (1971): 31–51.

43. Alleyne and Hall-Alleyne, "Language Maintenance," 55; Bilby, "Kromanti Dance," 65.

44. Currie, interview.

45. James Chambers, interview by the author, Accompong Town, St. Elizabeth, Jamaica, December 22, 2011.

46. Rowe and Ricketts, interview.

47. Ibid.

48. Carey, *Maroon Story*, 185.

49. Harris, "The True Traditions of my Ancestors," 39.

50. Ibid., 42.

51. Noel Prehay, "Welcome Remarks," (speech, Quao Day celebration, Charles Town, Jamaica, June 23, 2011).

52. Bilby, "Kromanti Dance," 54.

53. Ibid.

54. Olive Senior, *Encyclopedia of Jamaican Heritage* (St. Andrew, Jamaica: Twin Guinep, 2003), 357.

55. Konadu, *Akan Diaspora in the Americas*, 140.

56. Cawley, interview.
57. Ibid.
58. Chambers, interview.
59. Ibid.
60. Cawley, interview.
61. Harris N. Cawley, *The Sound of the Abeng: A Short Synopsis on the Accompong Maroons* (Accompong Town, Jamaica: Speedy Prints, 1986), 8.
62. Senior, *Encyclopedia of Jamaican Heritage*, 341.
63. Carey, *Maroon Story*, 182.
64. Cawley, interview.
65. Hansley Reid, interview by author, Accompong Town, St. Elizabeth, Jamaica, December 21, 2011.
66. Williams, interview.
67. Cawley, interview.
68. Harris, "Spirit of Nanny."
69. Prehay, "Introductory Remarks."
70. Ibid.
71. Bilby, *True-Born Maroon*, 480.
72. Senior, *Encyclopedia of Jamaican Heritage*, 357.
73. David McFadden, "Caribbean Maroons Hope Tourism Can Save Their Culture," Bloomberg Businessweek, July 10, 2012, accessed December 4, 2012, http://www.businessweek.com/ap/2012-07-10/caribbean-Maroons-hope-tourism-can-save-culture#p2.
74. McFarlane, *Cudjoe of Jamaica*, 84.
75. Carey, *Maroon Story*, 176.
76. MacFarlane, *Cudjoe of Jamaica*, 24.
77. Katherine Dunham and Ted Cook, *Katherine Dunham's Journey to Accompong* (New York: Henry Holt, 1946), 44.
78. "Jamaicans Have Roots in Ghana," *Afro-American* (Baltimore), August 13, 1960.
79. Laura Tanna, *Jamaican Folk Tales and Oral Histories* (Kingston: Institute of Jamaica Publications, 1984), 93.
80. Cawley, *Sound of the Abeng*, 6.
81. Reid, interview.
82. Carey, *Maroon Story*, 185.
83. Jacqueline Cogdell DjeDje, "Remembering Kojo: History, Music, and Gender in the January Sixth Celebration of the Jamaican Accompong Maroons," *Black Music Research Journal* 18, no. 1/2 (1998): 79.
84. Rowe and Ricketts, interview.
85. DjeDje, "Remembering Kojo," 100.
86. Ibid.
87. Dunham and Cook, *Katherine Dunham's Journey*, 86.
88. Kenneth M. Bilby, *Music of the Maroons of Jamaica* (New York: Folkways Records, 1981), 10.
89. Chambers, interview.

90. Harris, "Spirit of Nanny."

91. Bilby, *Music of the Maroons of Jamaica*, 3.

92. McFarlane, *Cudjoe of Jamaica*, 22.

93. Dallas, *History of the Maroons*, 89; Dunham and Cook, *Katherine Dunham's Journey*, 54.

94. The Abeng can be found among the Maroons of Suriname and French Guyana as well.

95. Reid, interview.

96. Rowe and Ricketts, interview; Bilby, *Music of the Maroons of Jamaica*, 3; Werner Zips, *Nanny's Asafo Warriors: The Jamaican Maroons' African Experience* (Kingston: Ian Randle, 2011), xix; Bilby, "Kromanti Dance," 56.

97. DjeDje, "Remembering Kojo," 84.

98. Konadu, *Akan Diaspora in the Americas*, 151.

99. Senior, *Encyclopedia of Jamaican Heritage*, 217.

100. Zips, *Nanny's Asafo Warriors*, 71.

101. Rachel Jackson, "The Trans-Atlantic Journey of Gumbé: Where and Why Has It Survived?" *African Music*, 9 (2012): 128.

102. Ibid., 139.

103. Bilby, "Music of the Maroons of Jamaica," 3; Sterling, interview.

104. Currie, interview.

105. "Fashionable Maroons," *Jamaica Gleaner* (Kingston), January 14, 2011, D5; Keril Wright, "Accompong Town Maroons Celebrate 271 Years of Freedom," *Jamaica Observer* (Kingston), January 8, 2009, accessed December 4, 2012, http://www.jamaicaobserver.com/pfversion/144575_Accompong-Town-Maroons-celebrate-271-years-of-freedom.

106. Currie, interview.

107. "Maroon Stories Artfully Etched in Wood," *Jamaica Gleaner* (Kingston), June 30, 2013, accessed March 12, 2013, http://jamaica-gleaner.com/gleaner/20130630/arts/arts1.html.

108. Dede Martin, *Asante Nse̱mfua Nkyere̱ase̱e̱ Nwoma = Twi Dictionary* (Tema, Ghana: Aburuburo Nkosua Series, 2010).

109. Ibid.

110. "Spirit Possession in Afro-Jamaican Religions and the Kromanti Play," African Caribbean Institute/Jamaica. Memory Bank, accessed March 12, 2013, http://acij-ioj.org.jm/spirit-possession-in-afro-jamaican-religions-and-the-kromanti-play/.

111. Rowe and Ricketts, interview.

112. Norma Rowe-Edwards, *My Father Said: A Story about the Accompong Maroons 1655–1738* (Riviera Beach, FL: Emerge Publishing Group, 2011), 79.

113. Accompong Traditional Medicinal Creative Group and Youth Project, *Maroon Traditional Medicine* (Accompong Town, St. Elizabeth, Jamaica: NP, 1994), 8.

114. Rowe and Ricketts, interview.

115. Rowe and Ricketts, interview; "Renewing the JA/Ghana Link," *Jamaica Gleaner* (Kingston), July 31, 1997.

4

Collective Consciousness

We are one family.

—Deputy Colonel Melville Currie of Accompong Town Maroon Community[1]

Introduction

IT IS IMPORTANT TO EXPLORE collective consciousness as it relates to Jamaican Maroon communities and the workings of the African Diaspora.[2] Then we can comprehend how claims of origin are not only enunciated but used to make particular linkages, internally among the Maroons themselves and externally with other people of African descent worldwide. Developing on previous thoughts, it is possible to see how the common experience of black abjection and ideas of a common African origin are used to build collective consciousness.

The notion of collective consciousness is produced out of a shared recognition of common conditions and experiences. It is common recognition of likeness across diversity. As Jacqueline Nassy Brown correctly argues, diasporic people "recognize themselves as being of like kind—as sharing some basis of identity—even if they express distinct, sometimes, contrary, histories, and experiences in relation to it."[3] As a result, the African Diaspora engages different identities, cultures, and social formations worldwide. Solidarity consciousness emerges out of the constitution of collective defensive and resistance against the condition of black abjection. It is a means of peoples finding "some ground, some place, some position on which to stand."[4] It is the idea of common origin that struggles against violent hegemonic power that produced collective consciousness. It is produced by the very global forces that refuse acknowledgment of black belonging to civilized humanity and the material conditions that result from such refusal.[5] In other words, the abjection of black peoples produced a great desire to identify roots in Africa, leading to the building of collective consciousness.

Maroons' critical practice and ideological view of their claim to African origin thus serve as the source underpinning their linkages to Africa, allowing them to connect to other peoples of African descent in Jamaica, the rest of the Americas, and Africa; their claims to African origin are important for diasporic articulation of collective consciousness.

Among Maroon Communities

It is important to note that the community of Maroons extends beyond those individuals who live at present in the physical Maroon settlements. The Maroon community is comprised of the ancestors (as in spirits), the "born" (living), and the "unborn" (future offspring).[6] The ancestors who originated in Africa are the foundation of the community. The community includes individuals who claim their origin in these African ancestors and can trace it back. It also consists of Maroons who are connected to Maroon families throughout Jamaica and the world in the past, present, and future. Maroon identity exists across time and place. It is about a memory that challenges the prevailing discourse, pedagogy, and knowledge.

The Maroons see themselves figuratively (and phenomenologically) as one big family. In the east (Windward Maroons), the Charles Town, Moore Town, and Scot's Hall Maroons all view themselves as Nanny *pikibo*, "children of Nanny" in the Kromanti language, Nanny being the sister of Kojo and Accompong. In the west (Leeward Maroons), the Accompong Maroons acknowledge the other groups of Maroons as brothers and sisters coming from the same original Africans and Maroons during the Spanish colonization of the island.

As in the case of Accompong, Kindah is both a place in central Accompong Town and a concept of place. Accompong Maroons define *Kindah* as an African word meaning "we are one family."[7] The physical place called Kindah is where the different groups of Africans of different ethnic origins, including the Asante, Kromanti, and Kongolese, came together as one family. As Melville Currie asserts:

> While the war was going on and the division was there, they [Maroons] had problems. So, under the [Kindah] Tree all tribes met and there they pricked the arches of their hand, like they would have done in Africa, and they all drank the blood in the name of peace and brotherhood. Hence, the name Kindah: "We are one family."[8]

In Accompong Town, Kindah is important in building solidarity among different groups of peoples of African origin in the community. For the Maroons, this was beyond a strategic alliance: community-building in a claimed common origin in Africa was a means of forming unity. According to Rowe-Edwards, anywhere Maroons meet it is considered Kindah. It does not matter whether they meet in Accompong Town, Kingston, or New York.[9]

Some Maroons even go further and link most of the Accompong Maroon families to the Rowe family, the community's largest family. They argue that the Rowes are direct descendants of Nanny, Kojo, and Accompong (all individuals said to be Akan). According to the former secretary of state Mann O. Rowe, both Kojo and Nanny were part of the Rowe family. He claims that the other large families, such as the Wrights, Reids, Crosses, and Fosters, are related to the Rowe family as well.[10] The universality and common acceptance of this notion that "We are one family" was reflected directly in the words of Lawrence Rowe, whose duty it was to represent the community to its visitors.[11] Ann-Marie Hutchinson, a community council member, believes that there were originally twelve Rowe brothers, which could explain the sizeable number of Rowes in the community.[12] Regardless of the number of Rowes, for the Maroons of Accompong, what is important is that the Rowes have become the symbolic center in the discourse of common descent and its link to African origin which has become one means of solidarity consciousness for the Maroons.

Maroons' collective identity is similar to lineage-based notions of belonging that are often linked to African ethnic/linguistic claims of origin. According to the former Colonel Cawley (1984–1988), you are Maroon by blood, and all Maroons are descendants of the original Maroons of Accompong Town.[13] Also, former Colonel Cawley states that anyone who can prove that he or she has Maroon blood is a Maroon.[14] For Accompong community member Ikamellia Foster, anybody born in Accompong Town within the Maroon family is a Maroon. She also includes their descendants, who may be from or outside of the settlement.[15]

In this regard, Maroons claim a clan-based system that they deem is African. It is significant as a basis for challenging statist authority and for justifying alternative forms of organization not instantiated in the nation-state. It demonstrates how Maroon identity is constituted as an alternative form of organizing that can extend across the nation-state's borders.

It is important to note that blood ties and physical space are significant as manifestations of unity. In the process of community building, Maroons advance collective consciousness among themselves as a group, accomplished within and across the four communities of Jamaica.

Among African Descendants

The use of origin is also a critical practice, deployed to make linkages to other peoples of African descent. As Colin Palmer rightly postulates, Diasporas are "symbolic communities and political constructs," in which members tend to "possess a sense of shared identity that transcends geographic boundaries."[16] Maroons recognize their connection to other peoples of African descent.

Claims to origin in Africa and their enunciation play a central and critical boundary-defining role for inclusion in the African Diaspora. What is important is that the claims to origin in Africa enunciated in various ways are what link Maroons to other communities of people making similar claims. Indeed, the significance of the claims relates to recognition that may be seen at times as "solidarity" and "unity," building collective consciousness.

Different groups of African descent phenomenologically articulate Diaspora in emphasizing collective consciousness in different ways. But the point is that the enunciations of African origin are central to recognizing linkages. Maroons position themselves as authentic holders of a "deeper root" of African heritage in the Western Hemisphere by identifying a specific place of origin. As Maroons interpret it, their communities act as unique sites to further connect and share consciousness of African values and cultural practices. Linkages are produced in and through mutually recognized enunciations, including those related to African origin. Linkages are produced because they are recognized as enunciations of blackness, which is understood to be based on the rejection to black abjection and acceptance of African origin.

Maroons have used the settlements as sites of enactment of solidarity consciousness and community-building. In the last few decades, a range of Maroon communities' activities has appealed to peoples of African descent. These moments of enactment of diasporic articulation of collective consciousness vary from year to year, depending on the community's leadership at any given time. The most popular occurrences are the annual Maroon Independence Day celebrations, community tours, and conferences. The importance of these is the role of the Maroons as signifying figures of blackness.

Maroons beckon people, especially those of African descent, to come and explore authentic African roots and celebrate successes in resisting black abjection. This may very well be Maroons' own strategic adaptation to globalization, but it is through the articulation of Diaspora that this is made possible. As articulation (as in connecting), Diaspora produces the conditions that undergird the motivations for these moments: the desire to see authentic African cultural practices and forms. Globalization and the tourist industry are important material conditions that allow the circulation of black unity, or what it is to be part of the African Diaspora.

Shared consciousness and claimed African traditions can be experienced in all Maroon communities. In the positioning of sites for diasporic articulation, Charles Town has been the most visible of the three Windward Maroon communities. Nevertheless, the other two, Moore Town and Scot's Hall, still have annual Independence Day celebrations.

About building solidarity with other people of African descent, Keith Lumsden, chairman of the Maroon Council of Charles Town, asserts: "We're trying to get our people to reconnect with their African roots, to show them that it's a wonderful thing."[17] This outreach is not just for other Jamaicans but also for peoples of African descent in general. What is enunciated is an authentic African practice that has been combined with tourist and marketing technologies in the global circuits of blackness. The Maroons represent the materialization of authentic African roots. However, it must be noted that the connections to tourism do not invalidate the community practice of forming shared consciousness, although they may affect it.

In 2011, the *Jamaican Information Service* (*JIS*), the country's information-provider agency, stated that with the nation's school systems attempting to make black history an important part of the school curriculum, Maroon communities are "the perfect opportunity for students to dig deep into their past, to learn about aspects of the Jamaican cultural heritage."[18] Hence, visitors to Maroon communities such as Charles Town are encouraged. The JIS indicates as examples of the richness of Maroon communities for cultural development:

> Visitors to the Charles Town Maroons' Museum and Safu Yard in the Buff Bay Valley, Portland, can get the thrilling experience of tracing the footsteps of their ancestors into the hills, as they ascend the Sambo Hill Hiking Trail. As a practical re-enactment of the Literature Text "The Young Warriors," a story depicting the struggles of some young Maroons, approximately 200 students and teachers of Meadowbrook High School, Kingston, embarked on the historical adventure, as they grasped the opportunity to retrace a part of their history on Friday, February 11. Excited about the journey to Sambo Hill, the students and their teachers, led by enthusiastic tour guides, carefully maneuvered the challenging terrain with its slippery rocks and damp vegetation. Literature

> teacher at Meadowbrook High School Tristan Brown said it was a good practical experience for the students. "It was designed to give them a direct purposeful experience, as they recounted the history of the Maroons." She said although the terrain was challenging, it was important for them to understand the struggles of their ancestors, as it taught them to be more appreciative of the sacrifices they made.[19]

The accommodation of African origin in Jamaican national narratives is highlighted with references to the Maroon presence.

There have been many public events in Charles Town over the years. In the last ten years, the Charles Town Maroons have had the annual Charles Town Maroon Conference and Festival in the summer, with a number of different activities. The date in late June coincides with the anniversary of Quao's signing of the Treaty with the British.[20] As another example, in October 2011, the former Colonel Lumsden (2004–2015) of Charles Town organized a weekend retreat with Capoeira and Maroon performance, linking the town and the Capoeira practice through a celebration of forms of African resistance.[21]

Many Maroon leaders of Accompong have used their administrations to highlight collective consciousness with Africa and other peoples of African descent. For instance, in 1998, former Colonel Meredith Rowe (1993–1998) of Accompong announced in the *Jamaica Gleaner* newspaper:

> I also want from the Maroon perspective to remind all of Jamaica as well as the wider regions that the Accompong Maroon State in Saint Elisabeth has taken the decision to hold three major events each year. All these are of cultural and historical importance, carrying messages of the most effective figures of the Diaspora of the Maroons of Jamaica. These events [unlike the annual Kojo Day celebration] will carry no entry fee, so come with all cultural skills, be it *kumina*, drumming, dancing, *gerreh*, *myal*, revival, skit, acrobatic skills, folklore or even Anancy story: they will be all welcome.[22]

Accompong Maroons believe that encouraging others to celebrate with them is a great opportunity for Jamaicans to learn more about the traditions of their African foreparents.[23]

In Jamaica and beyond, people, especially those of African descent, are encouraged to come and celebrate with the Maroons a unique, authentic, and independent "African" community in the Americas. Once again, according to former Colonel Meredith Rowe of Accompong Town, in Jamaica, "The Maroon community is still the only significant organised Black link with our African past."[24] All peoples of African descent of course have links to an "African past," but some Maroons argue that they do a better job of preserving such links. Moreover, in 1999, former Colonel Sidney Peddie (1998–2009) of Accompong referred to their settlement as the "cradle of our culture" in Jamaica.[25] Here, Maroons state the provocative claim that their connections to African origin make them central to the Jamaican core culture (which, they imply, is African) that unites them with all Afro-Jamaicans. Furthermore, Bev Carey reports that black Jamaicans wanting to express their African connections regularly go to Accompong Town celebrations: "performances" of African origin.[26] Various people enunciate blackness differently, even those with explicit claims to African origin, such as the Maroons. What is being enunciated here is a relatively unsullied form of Africanity.

Maroons of Accompong make links with specific groups of black people or black people in general at various conferences. In 2006, the Surinamese Maroon leader Kenrick Cairo participated in a conference in Accompong Town discussing concerns of interest to all Maroons under the theme: "Restoring, Preserving and Protecting Our Heritage."[27] In 2007, Maroons, under the leadership of former Colonel Peddie (1998–2009), participated in the Joseph Project, which commemorated the 200th anniversary of abolishing the slave trade. The project aimed to establish links with the descendants of enslaved Africans worldwide to work towards healing the wounds of slavery.[28] In October 2012, the Accompong Maroons explored links with other Maroons and Afro-Jamaicans at a conference that had the theme "The Africans in Jamaica—Safeguarding Intangible Cultural Heritage of the Maroons for Democracy, Governance & Development."[29] In all of these conferences, diasporic linkages are made through claims to origin in Africa.

Another type of diasporic articulation and building of consciousness is through community tours of Accompong, in which Maroons encourage shared consciousness with other peoples of African descent visiting their communities throughout the year. It is under the recasting of heritage tourism that this commemoration of shared African traditions is being positioned. Accompong Town is the most visited of the Maroon communities, with visits virtually daily. Maroons promote visiting to share just about all of their traditions, the African cultural traditions being most emphasized. Visitors and sojourners are taken mainly to the seven "African-influenced" cultural sites in Accompong Town: Accompong Museum; Sealed Grounds; the Asante, Kromanti, and Kongo burial ground; Herbal (Asante) Hut; Kindah; Kojo Monument (also a Sealed Ground); and Old Town. Additional activities include excursions into the wider Cockpit Country areas through hiking, bird watching, and caving. Furthermore, arrangements can be made to explore other Maroon traditions, most linked to Africa, such as herb lore, crafts (especially drum-making), story-telling, and local foods.

However, the most popular moment of diasporic articulation of collective consciousness building happens on Kojo Day every January 6th. In Accompong Town, although traditions are practiced throughout the year, forms that express African-ness are displayed above all in the annual Sixth of January celebration. Most Maroons consider their practices at the celebration to be sharing of solidarity of being African. This is how the former Colonel M. L. Wright (1967–1984 and 1988–1993) describes the celebration:

> The greatest community event is the festival which is held every January to celebrate Kojo's victory over the British which led to the treaty. This festival is planned to coincide with Kojo's birthday and celebrates Kojo's remarkable leadership and the sacrifice he made fighting for his people in this wild and rugged Cockpit country for so many long, dreary years. The celebrations also remind all Maroons of the hard days of the struggle to maintain their freedom. Maroons reunite in their dedication to stand firm on their traditional values for freedom, liberty, and respect for human dignity.[30]

Although this statement expresses many different ideas, African heritage is an important component, as are the freedom and self-determination central to all independence narratives everywhere. There is also the element of challenges to black abjection in the British defeat and the treaty that secured sovereignty. Thus, the Maroons' signifying role is not confined to Africanity and shared collective consciousness, although they are important.

Many Accompong Maroons believe that the celebration started in the late 1730s right after the victory against the British and has continued up to the present-day.[31] Apart from a two- or three-year absence, this celebration does seem to have occurred in Accompong Town for most of the twentieth and twenty-first centuries. There have been accounts of the celebration by several observers over the years. Henry Rowe, the colonel in the 1920s and 1930s, mentions that the celebration was in existence in the early 1900s.[32] In the mid-1930s, Zora Neale Hurston, on her visit to Accompong Town, said that the celebration was still one of the few major events in the community.[33] In the late 1970s, the anthropologist Kenneth Bilby noted that he saw thousands of outsiders at the annual Sixth of January celebration in Accompong Town.[34] As the years go by, the figures have fluctuated, but there has been a general increase in numbers: 17,000 in 1992, 14,000 in 1998, 17,000 in 2002, and 25,000 in 2007.[35]

As has been practiced over the last few decades, and as described by former Colonel M. L. Wright, the celebration is divided into four or five major parts.[36] According to former Colonel Cawley (1984–1988), the celebration begins at Kindah, the area in which the Kindah Tree is located, where food is prepared.

> Maroons are very peculiar in their cooking. No women are allowed to cook on that day. Only two types of food are used: yellow yam and plantain. No food that

is white in appearance can be used. This is done as a tradition which we inherited from our forefathers. For the meat, no female animals or birds are used. The meat is pork and it must be boar. Roast birds are always used. On the early morning of the celebration, the pig is killed. A large fire is made and covered with green leaves. The pig is put on top of the leaves, and then finally covered with more leaves. The green leaves are properly heated so the moisture will penetrate the hairy body of the pig. This will allow easy removal of the hair by scraping with a sharp knife. The pork is cooked in large containers. No salt is allowed to be used. The food is still cooked without salt today. Many attest to the fact that the food does taste fresh, even though it is cooked without salt. All the main activities of the celebration take place at Kindah, the original dancing ground of the Maroons.[37]

There is singing, drumming, and dancing throughout the day but especially in the morning. The practices reported by former Colonel Cawley in the 1980s continue to this day:

The main activities during the celebration are dancing, singing, and eating. The dancing and singing are done simultaneously, accompanied by the playing of the Gumbé and the blowing of the horn. The horn is also known as the "Abeng." The "Gumbé" is a kind of Drum that is played with the hands. Karamante is the name given to the songs that are sung. The songs are very suggestive of the whole occasion. Some of the songs are . . . 1) Law hold already oh, Law hold oh; 2) Fanny Mall a come oh, clear road oh; 3) Nina (Nanny) mi a tome, A'Juma tek yu yard; 4) Shalla kill a man aye; and other songs which depict their culture strongly. Different songs are used for different purposes.[38]

In Maroon communities, singing, drumming, and dancing serve as a means of connecting and communicating with the ancestors (the most powerful ones being African). Colonel Williams (2009–present) believes that when you dance, the ancestors dance through you.[39] Also, the ancestors talk to you and you talk back to them.[40] Furthermore, according to Lance Ricketts, at the Kindah Tree around January 6th, through dancing, the ancestors such as Kojo and Accompong talk to or through them.[41] According to Lawrence Rowe, historically, especially at the Kojo Day celebration, when the Maroons come together, they dance in a traditional African way.[42]

The second part of the annual event is a visit to Old Town. On that day, only "full-blooded" Maroons are allowed to visit the sacred ground where Kojo, Accompong, and other past Maroon leaders are believed to be buried.[43] In this, the group of Maroons take a portion of the cooked food and feed the ancestors before anyone else is allowed to eat the food. According to former Colonel M. L. Wright (1967–1984 and 1988–1993),

It is during the preparation for the visit to the sacred grounds that the sprinkling of the sacred grounds with rum and the pouring of libation takes place. During

> that time there is the preparation of the food to be carried to feed the spirits of the Maroon heroes. The food includes pork as the meat and boiled yam. At the graves of the heroes, in addition to pouring libation (which among the Accompong Maroons is basically the sprinkling of rum over the sacred grounds), food is thrown around the area. A tense moment comes at the place when the visiting Maroons must have a period of spiritual communication with their ancestors, but must be preceded by a long period of silence and mediation—what among them is referred to as a "reasoning session."[44]

The third part of the day is the return march to the Kindah Tree, where the ritual food was prepared.[45] At this point, the returnees join the other group of performers at Kindah with the singing, drumming, and dancing. According to former Colonel Cawley, "After the party returns, the order will be given by the supervisor to share the food for the people. The food is shared on banana leaves. Anyone who desires to participate can do so."[46]

The last major site of the celebration is at a place called Parade Ground. But now, or at least during the celebrations in 2012, 2013, 2015, and 2018, before going to Parade Ground there is a large procession through the town. Formerly, the Town Square was used instead of Parade Ground, as former Colonel M. L. Wright (1967–1984 and 1988–1993) states:

> The last part of the celebrations takes place in the modern Accompong Town at the monument erected in honour of Kojo. That is the part of the celebrations in which Maroon and non-Maroon come in contact and share in the merrymaking. Traditional Maroon food, rum, Maroon traditional *gombey* drumming, music, and dance as well as family re-unions—all against the backdrop of the achievements of the past—are the order of the day. The *abeng* sounds from time to time, sending messages to the Maroons and all who can understand. In recent years, the practice has been to invite a distinguished personality to grace the occasion, and this represents the extension of good will to the larger Jamaican and international public.[47]

At Parade Ground, speeches and performances are presented. As former Colonel Cawley (1984–1988) mentions, "The Colonel will then give his address. The speech is not long and usually it outlines some of the past programmes as well as gives a projection of what is to be done in the months ahead. Others are allowed to give their views. After the speeches are concluded, the night session will be devoted to several dances."[48] The speeches tend to be filled with enunciations of African connections.

Maroon communities, particularly Accompong Town, have served as a major site of linkages between groups of African-descended peoples. The annual number of visitors or sojourners to Maroon communities has increased from hundreds to tens of thousands.[49] Also, each Maroon community has dozens to over a thousand visitors annually. According to newspaper accounts and the logbooks of Accompong Town, in the last few years the visitors of African descent have come from Jamaica, North America (the United States and Canada), the Caribbean (Bahamas, Barbados, and Haiti), Latin America (Belize, Colombia, and Suriname), Africa (Ghana, Kenya, and Nigeria), and Europe (the United Kingdom).[50] The vast majority are of African descent, and many come in solidarity to celebrate Maroon culture, believing they share a common origin with the communities. The communities are sites of sharing of diasporic experiences, histories, and cultures supported by arguments of common origin in Africa.

Not surprisingly, the largest population of visitors as a distinct category of people are Afro-Jamaicans. They include a range of governmental officials, from the heads of state, such as prime ministers P. J. Patterson, Portia Simpson Miller, and Andrew Holness, to officials in minor governmental offices.[51] Also, cultural artists and performers, such as the Stone Love musical entertainers and Sizzla Kalonji, have visited the communities.[52] Throughout the decades, local groups, such as the Hartford Culture Group and the Mighty Beeston Mento Band, have performed folk songs and dances. These performances are from the shared tradition of Maroons, black Jamaicans, and other people of African descent.[53]

Many high-profile people of non-Jamaican descent have visited as well. This includes a sizeable population of African Americans, including such well-known ones as the rapper Snoop Dogg and the U. S. Ambassador Pamela Bridgewater.[54]

From the Caribbean, many black leaders have attended, including Surinamese Maroons. For instance, in Accompong Town in 1998, a five-member Surinamese delegation led by the Paramount Chief of the Matawai nation, Nana Lafanti Abone, attended the Kojo Day celebration. The two communities, essentially re-articulating Diaspora, at that time discussed possible trade, cultural, and other exchanges with each other.[55]

Black leaders from Africa, many diplomats, and even heads of state, such as Jerry Rawlings of Ghana, and an heir to the Ethiopian throne, Prince Ermias Sahle-Selassie, have visited Maroon communities.[56] Nigerian High Commissioners, including Adebowele Adefuye, Ruffus Satunase, and Olatokunboh Kamson, have been fixtures at various Maroon communities' celebrations.[57] In 1992, the Nigerian High Commissioner, Professor Emmanuel Ugochukwu, speaking at the Accompong annual celebration and acknowledging the connection with Maroons and other peoples of African descent, called for unity of all black people as the answer to the problems that black people face.[58] In 2012, the Ghanaian Dr. Kwame Boafo, United Nations director and representative for the Caribbean Kingston Cluster Office, was in attendance for the Kojo Day celebration in solidarity with Maroons.[59] In 2018, Dr. Arikana Chihombori-Quao, Permanent Representative of the African Union Representational Mission to the United States, spoke at the Kojo Day celebration in Accompong Town.[60]

Other non-political figures attend these celebrations. In the late 1990s, Nigerian dancers performed cultural song, music, dance, and poetry at the Accompong's Kojo Day celebration.[61] In 2015, the Ghanaian traditional Asante Priest Nana Kwaku Bonsam joined the Kojo Day celebration, called for all African people to unite, and remarked that most Jamaicans and members of the Asante people have a similar culture.[62] Clearly, Maroon communities have become sites of pilgrimage for African-descended peoples to share African heritage.

The visits and events create significant moments of diasporic articulation. For instance, in 1991, the annual Kojo Day celebration was dedicated to Nelson Mandela, contributing and giving verbal support to the Anti-Apartheid struggle.[63] In 2007, at the Kojo Day celebration, the former Colonel Prehay (c. 1983–2016) of Scot's Hall called for reparations to all Africans who suffered from the effects of 500 years of slavery, linking them to the genocidal acts against the Jews in the twentieth century.[64] Such moments commemorate the common experience of black abjection and resistance to it.

These various foreign leaders who have attended the events collectively speak on behalf of tens of thousands of people in Africa and the Americas, bringing greetings from their people and celebrating their connection to the Maroon communities and their achievements. These contacts of peoples of African descent are more than mere expressions of camaraderie: rather, they are exchanges of ideas about what it is to belong to the African Diaspora. In other words, these are particular examples of the manner in which Diaspora is a process of constant re-articulation, incorporating new and changing forms of black enunciations and developing, expanding, and intensifying linkages, a result of new conditions of black circulation facilitated by post-colonialism and globalization. The work of these leaders and cultural ambassadors is paramount in how the circulation of knowledge of marronage and its importance as a signifying trope of Africanity and connection occurs.

Such celebrations and festive events in these communities are similar to festive events among other black peoples in the Americas and Africa that make specific claims to African authenticity and relate to origins. Maroons link these events to their African roots, shared consciousness, and common experience of abjection with all African descendants.

Although the settlements are the main sites of diasporic articulation of collective consciousness, Maroons visit numerous sites outside their communities. Maroon leaders, cultural performers, and other individuals have gone to other parts of Jamaica and beyond to share their African heritage, including to Barbados, Canada, Trinidad, and the United States.[65]

North America is a popular destination for Maroons to share their culture. In the United States in 1992, at the Smithsonian Institution Festival of American Folklife, Maroons from Colombia, French Guyana, Jamaica, Mexico, Suriname, and the United States were brought together: a moment for Maroons to express their cultures and create dialogue about diasporic linkages based on common experience of black abjection and claims of origin.[66] In 2009, the Charles Town Maroons conducted workshops showcasing their drumming, language, and storytelling traditions in Ottawa, Toronto, and Nova Scotia in Canada.[67] More recently, in 2016, the Granny Nanny Cultural Group of Moore Town Maroon community did a two-month tour in the United States with performances and speeches about their oral history.[68]

The most significant travel may have been to Ghana. In 1997, Maroons connected with Ghana through Colonel Meredith Rowe (1993–1998) and a small Maroon delegation that visited and met with government officials and some chiefs of the country. The Colonel also attended the Pan African Historical Theatre Festival (PANAFEST). According to him, the objective of PANAFEST, in line with many of the Maroons' goals, was to "develop a framework for the identification and analysis of issues and needs central to Africa's development and to the improvement of the quality of life of people of the entire continent and the Diaspora."[69] He attempted to establish partnerships with Ghana, including aiming to twin Akropong in Akuapem, Ghana, with Accompong.[70] As an acknowledgment of solidarity consciousness, Colonel Rowe said he was offered a Ghanaian passport and accepted the title of a paramount chief (and the honorary name Nana Kodwah Eduawah I), which came with the granting of assets, including property, suited to his office at a ceremony in his honor.[71]

Then in 2015, an Accompong Maroon delegation led by Colonel Williams (2009–present) made a three-day official visit to Ghana. There they met with the Asantehene (monarch of the Asante people), Otumfuo Osei Tutu II, and former President John Dramani Mahama.[72] The point is that Diaspora is constantly rearticulated.

Conclusion

Diaspora as articulation is manifested through various means. In different diasporic communities, there are different means of enunciating a shared black consciousness. Even in a given African diasporic community, these diasporic enunciations may change over time.

The Maroons have become significations of African authenticity and shared consciousness of not only the African past but of present and futures, too. The importance is not only that they make origin claims to Africa (all black people do as a condition of their blackness), but that Diaspora is reflected in the linkages and connections based on these enunciations of an authentic Africanity. These linkages have a material effect reflected in the pattern of circulation, both in visits to Maroon communities and in representatives of Maroons visiting outside the communities.

Through these moments and celebrations, mutual intangible benefits (such as a sense of black pride and fellowship) are derived from sharing cultural expression and art forms. They create a space to explore symbols, acts, and images of what it is to be part of the African Diaspora.

Africans participate and are increasingly involved in Diaspora forms of circulation, contributing to our ever-shifting understanding of blackness. These African interlocutors, no mere participants, include African leaders, diplomats, chiefs/kings, spiritualists, cultural artists, and tourists.

In many respects, Maroons' performative space constitutes a materialization of Diaspora articulation organized around the contesting of abjection, claims of African origin, the enunciation of blackness, shared consciousness, and black universal linkage. This is particularly evident in the rituals and ceremonies as well as the role of Maroon communities as heritage sites.

Notes

1. Melville Currie, interview by author, Accompong Town, St. Elizabeth, Jamaica, August 14, 2012.
2. Parts of this chapter were previously published in *Symbolism* and used with permission. Mario Nisbett, "African Diasporic Traditional Symbols and Claims," in *Rüdiger Ahrens, Florian Kläger*, Keith A. Sandiford and Klaus Stierstorfer (eds.) of *Symbolism: An International Annual of Critical Aesthetics*, Volume 16, Berlin, Germany: De Gruyter, 2016, 117–138.
3. J. N. Brown, "Black Europe and the African Diaspora: A Discourse on Location," in *Black Europe and the African Diaspora*, eds. Darlene Clark Hine, Trica Danielle Keaton, and Stephen Small (Urbana: University of Illinois Press, 2009), 202.
4. Stuart Hall, "Old and New Identities, Old and New Ethnicities," in *Theories of Race and Racism: A Reader*, eds. John Solomos and Les Back (London: Routledge, 2001), 148.
5. James Clifford, "Diasporas," *Cultural Anthropology* 9, no. 3 (1994): 312.
6. Ferron Williams, interview by author, Accompong Town, St. Elizabeth, Jamaica, January 7, 2012; Garfield Rowe, interview by author, Accompong Town, St. Elizabeth, Jamaica, January 10, 2013.

7. Norma Rowe-Edwards, *My Father Said: A Story about the Accompong Maroons 1655–1738* (Riviera Beach, FL: Emerge Publishing Group, 2011), 79.

8. Melvin Currie, interview by author, Accompong Town, St. Elizabeth, Jamaica, August 14, 2012.

9. Rowe-Edwards, *My Father Said*, 63.

10. Mann O. Rowe, interview by an unknown interviewer, undated, interview T265, African Caribbean Institute of Jamaica, Kingston, Jamaica.

11. Lawrence Rowe and Lance Ricketts, interview by author, Accompong Town, St. Elizabeth, Jamaica, January 8, 2012.

12. Ann-Marie Hutchinson, interview by author, Accompong Town, St. Elizabeth, Jamaica, December 28, 2011.

13. Harris Cawley, interview by author, Accompong Town, St. Elizabeth, Jamaica, August 01, 2012.

14. Ibid.

15. Ikamellia Foster, interview by author, Accompong Town, St. Elizabeth, Jamaica, December 30, 2011.

16. Colin A. Palmer, "Defining and Studying the Modern African Diaspora," *Journal of Negro History* 85, no. 1/2 (2000): 29.

17. "Blowing of Abeng to Highlight Maroon Celebrations," *JIS News* (Kingston), December 30, 2005, accessed December 4, 2012, http://jis.gov.jm/blowing-of-abeng-to-highlight-Maroon-celebrations/.

18. "Meadowbrook High Students Follow Nanny's Trail," *JIS News* (Kingston), February 18, 2011, accessed December 4, 2012, http://jis.gov.jm/meadowbrook-high-students-follow-nannys-trail-2/.

19. Ibid.

20. Charles Town Maroon Community, "Charles Town Maroon Community," accessed May 29, 2020. http://www.maroons-jamaica.com/q/index.php/home.

21. Charles Campbell, "Caan Ketch Quakuh . . .," *Jamaica Observer* (Kingston), June 8, 2010, accessed March 12, 2013, http://www.jamaicaobserver.com/Caan-Ketch-Quakuh.

22. Meredith Rowe, "Maroons Salute Emancipation Heroes," *Jamaica Gleaner* (Kingston), July 30, 1998.

23. "Blowing of Abeng."

24. "Maroons Concerned about Development of Kings House Lands," *Jamaica Gleaner* (Kingston), November 1, 1995.

25. Pamella Fae Jackson, "Tourist Trek to Accompong," *Jamaica Gleaner* (Kingston), January 14, 1999.

26. Bev Carey, *The Maroon Story: The Authentic and Original History of the Maroons in the History of Jamaica, 1490–1880* (Gordon Town, Jamaica: Agouti Press, 1997), ix.

27. "Maroon Homecoming," *Jamaica Observer* (Kingston), December 25, 2005, accessed December 4, 2012, http://www.jamaicaobserver.com/pfversion/95332_Maroon-homecoming; Garfield Myers, "Maroons Hold 'Mother of all Celebrations' at 268th Annual Festival," *Jamaica Observer* (Kingston), January 8, 2006, accessed

December 4, 2012, http://www.jamaicaobserver.com/pfversion/96134_Maroons-hold--mother-of-all-celebrations--at-268th-annual-festival.

28. Myers, "Maroons Hold 'Mother of all Celebrations.'"

29. "International Conference to Examine Life and Culture of Maroons," *Jamaica Observer* (Kingston), October 15, 2012, accessed March 12, 2013, http://www.jamaicaobserver.com/pfversion/International-conference-to-examine-life-and-culture-of-Maroons; "Young Maroons Upbeat about the Future," *JIS News* (Kingston), December 27, 2012, accessed March 12, 2013, http://jis.gov.jm/young-Maroons-upbeat-about-the-future/.

30. Colonel Martin-Luther Wright, "Accompong Maroons of Jamaica," in *Maroon Heritage Archaeological, Ethnographic, and Historical Perspectives,* ed. E. Kofi Agorsah (Barbados: Canoe Press, 1994), 68.

31. Currie, interview; Jacqueline Cogdell DjeDje, "Remembering Kojo: History, Music, and Gender in the January Sixth Celebration of the Jamaican Accompong Maroons," *Black Music Research Journal* 18, no. 1/2 (1998): 91.

32. Wright, "Accompong Maroons of Jamaica," 70; "Maroons Celebrate: Bicentenary of Freedom," *Jamaica Gleaner* (Kingston), March 5, 1938.

33. DjeDje, "Remembering Kojo," 92–93.

34. Ibid.

35. Conroy Walker, "Accompong Celebrations a Success Despite Concerns about Event Date," *Jamaica Observer* (Kingston), January 12, 2002, accessed January 25, 2014, http://www.jamaicaobserver.com/pfversion/19578_Accompong-celebrations-a-success-despite-concerns-about-event-date.

36. Wright, "Accompong Maroons of Jamaica," 69.

37. Harris N. Cawley, *The Sound of the Abeng: A Short Synopsis on the Accompong Maroons* (Accompong Town, Jamaica: Speedy Prints, 1986), 8.

38. Ibid.

39. Williams, interview.

40. Ibid.

41. Rowe and Rickets, interview.

42. Ibid.

43. Wright, "Accompong Maroons of Jamaica," 69.

44. Ibid.

45. Ibid.

46. Cawley, *Sound of the Abeng,* 8.

47. Wright, "Accompong Maroons of Jamaica," 69.

48. Cawley, *Sound of the Abeng,* 8.

49. "African Inspiration at Maroon Celebration," *Jamaica Gleaner* (Kingston), January 11, 2010; Campbell, "Caan Ketch Quakuh."

50. "A Colourful Maroon Celebration," *Jamaica Gleaner* (Kingston), January 8, 1998; "Maroons Celebrate—Mark 274th Anniversary Signing," *Jamaica Gleaner* (Kingston), January 14, 2012; "No Filming of Maroons' 259th Anniversary," *Jamaica Gleaner* (Kingston), January 6, 1998.

51. "Prime Minister Hails Accompong Town Maroons," *JIS News* (Kingston), January 07, 2019, accessed March 14, 2020, https://jis.gov.jm/prime-minister-hails-accompong-town-maroons/.

52. Ibid.

53. Myers, "Maroons Hold 'Mother of all Celebrations'"; Garfield Myers, "Maroons Unite in Defence of Cockpit Country," *Jamaica Observer* (Kingston), January 8, 2007, accessed March 12, 2013, http://www.jamaicaobserver.com/pfversion/117619_Maroons-unite-in-defence-of-Cockpit-Country; "Holness Hails Accompong Town Maroons."

54. "Maroons Celebrate—Mark 274th Anniversary Signing."

55. "No Filming of Maroons'."

56. "Renewing the JA/Ghana Link"; "Prince Sahle-Selassie ends Visit," *Jamaica Observer* (Kingston), May 01, 2016, accessed March 27, 2020, http://www.jamaicaobserver.com/results/?text=Prince+Sahle-Selassie+ends+Visit&sa=GO.

57. "Respect Sacrifices of Forefathers," *Jamaica Gleaner* (Kingston), January 12, 1989; "Former Maroon Colonel Says Thanks," *Jamaica Gleaner* (Kingston), August 11, 1999; "Charles Town Maroons Celebrate Culture," *JIS News* (Kingston), June 30, 2011, accessed December 4, 2012, http://jis.gov.jm/charles-town-Maroons-celebrate-culture/; Garfield Myers, "Maroons Gather to Celebrate 275-Year-Old Peace Treaty," *Jamaica Observer* (Kingston), January 6, 2013, accessed March 12, 2013, http://www.jamaicaobserver.com/pfversion/January-6-come-again-_13322164.

58. "'Unity of Black Nations the Answer,'" *Jamaica Gleaner* (Kingston), January 10, 1992.

59. "Maroons Celebrate—Mark 274th Anniversary Signing."

60. "Accompong Celebrates 280 Years Since Maroon Peace Treaty," *Jamaica Gleaner* (Kingston), January 8, 2018 accessed 18 Jan. 2018, http://jamaica-gleaner.com/article/lead-stories/20180108/accompong-celebrates-280-years-Maroon-peace-treaty.

61. "A Colourful Maroon Celebration."

62. "Ashanti Priest Celebrates with Maroons in Accompong," *Jamaica Observer* (Kingston), January 11, 2015, accessed March 27, 2020, http://www.jamaicaobserver.com/news/Ashanti-priest-celebrates-with-Maroons-in-Accompong.

63. "Maroons to Honour Mandela," *Jamaica Gleaner* (Kingston), January 4, 1991.

64. Myers, "Maroons Hold 'Mother of all Celebrations.'"

65. "Maroons to Re-trace Footsteps of Ancestors," *JIS News* (Kingston), July 17, 2009, accessed March 12, 2013, http://jis.gov.jm/Maroons-to-re-trace-footsteps-of-ancestors/; "Canadians Learning About Maroon Culture," *JIS News* (Kingston), August 7, 2009, accessed March 12, 2013, http://jis.gov.jm/canadians-learning-about-Maroon-culture/.

66. Festival of American Folklife, *Festival of American Folklife: June 25–June 29; July 2– July 5* (Washington, DC: The Smithsonian Institution, 1992).

67. "Canadians Learning About Maroon Culture," *JIS News* (Kingston), August 7, 2009, accessed March 12, 2013, http://jis.gov.jm/canadians-learning-about-Maroon-culture/.

68. Paul H. Williams, “Granny Nanny Cultural Group tours USA,” *Jamaica Gleaner* (Kingston), August 24, 2016, accessed March 13, 2020, http://jamaica-gleaner.com/article/news/20160825/granny-nanny-cultural-group-tours-usa.

69. “J’can Delegation Participate in Panafest,” *Jamaica Gleaner* (Kingston), August 29, 1997.

70. “Accompong Maroons Reunited,” *Jamaica Gleaner* (Kingston), January 3, 1998.

71. “J’can Delegation Participate in Panafest”; “Ghana Confers Title on Maroon Leader,” *Jamaica Gleaner* (Kingston), January 6, 1998.

72. “Historical Meeting Between The Kingdom Of Ashanti And The Accompong Maroons In Jamaica,” *Modern Ghana*, May 02, 2016, accessed March 12, 2020, https://www.modernghana.com/news/689367/historical-meeting-between-the-kingdom-of-ashanti.html.

5

Sovereignty Claims

We [Maroons] are sovereign in our own right.

—Former Colonel Harris Cawley of
Accompong Town Maroon Community[1]

Introduction

IN THEIR OWN VOICE, Maroons situate themselves as sovereign communities that, through critical practice, struggle against the colonial and post-colonial Jamaican state. Their claims to sovereignty are rooted in both pre-colonial and current notions of sovereign African statehood and self-determination, challenging European ideas of black abjection and an African Hobbesian state of nature. Maroons assert the right to statehood as equal with the European colonial and metropolitan states. Through diasporic articulation and critical practice, the Maroon communities are able to make certain socio-political claims on territorial space. This is most evident in collective land rights and environmental views attributed to African roots that are linked to sovereignty.

Reviving African Statehood

The Maroons, from a phenomenological perspective, see themselves as a sovereign state. The founding of the state is traced back to its origin in Africa, a claim constantly reiterated by the general Maroon population and their leaders.

In Maroon oral history, the African chieftaincy or kingdom type of governing system was established by the Maroons during the founding of the communities in the sixteenth, seventeenth, and eighteenth centuries. As Bev Carey observes, the early Maroons re-created African communities with an Asante-like political system.[2] The Moore Town Maroon author Milton MacFarlane reinforces the role of African governing practice by arguing that "Kromanteen laws and customs" from West Africa were used in the organizing and governing of Maroon communities.[3] According to Colonel Wallace Sterling (1995–present) of Moore Town, Maroons had a long history of governing themselves, all the way back to Africa.[4] For former Colonel Frank Lumsden (2004–2015) of the Charles Town Maroons, their governing structure was based on an "Akan system."[5] Former Colonel Noel Prehay (c. 1983–2016) of the Scot's Hall Maroons states that the Maroons' political system came from their Asante ancestors.[6]

Maroons often proclaim that their governing system is similar to African chieftaincies. They argue that although the current official title of the head of the Maroon government is "colonel," his or her role bears some resemblance to that of an African chief. Deputy Colonel Melville Currie of Accompong states that the colonels were known as "chief" during the period of the war between the Maroons and the British in the seventeenth and early eighteenth centuries.[7] Further, although Accompong Town is ruled by a colonel, "you can call him the chief, as they were in Africa."[8] Former Deputy Colonel Norma Rowe-Edwards asserts that the "leaders were given the honorary title as Chief. I am not sure at what time the subsequent leaders were called Colonel, a Colonial title, but that is what the leader is called today."[9] According to former Colonel Prehay of Scot's Hall, the political system of the Maroons came from their Akan ancestors, but the title "colonel" did not, and although he uses the title, he sees himself more as a chief, which he believes is in line with his African ancestors' views.[10]

The Maroons claim that they are products of independent sovereign states that existed prior to their enslavement and that they deserve to be considered sovereign on the basis of this. These claims to a prior sovereign statehood and its form of political organization are used to reference (signify) that reality. The point is that it demonstrates the organizational bases upon which sovereign statehood rests. It is a perceived continuation of past African practice.

Interpreting Treaty Agreements

For the Jamaican Maroons, particularly the Accompong Maroons, the Treaties of 1739 with the British colonial authorities are viewed as formal recognition of Maroons' sovereignty. Mann O. Rowe stated that the Treaty is sacred and was agreed to between two sovereign powers in Jamaica.[11] According to former Colonel Wright (1967–1984 and 1988–1993), "the result of these treaties was to make the Maroons of Jamaica a free, independent self-governing group of people."[12]

It is important to note that the Maroons interpret the Treaty agreements from an African perspective that challenges the British one; hence, there are conflicting views on what the Treaties mean, as has recently come to light in Maroon studies. It has been traditionally thought that the Treaties should be understood essentially through the written documentation of the British. However, if we are to consider the Maroon perspective, we have to recognize that the Treaties were achieved through both written agreements and oath-taking agreements made through a blood ritual. The Maroon version, with its interpretation, is conveyed through oral history. From the British perspective, the written Treaties were signed with the symbol of an "X" by the two Maroon groups who authorized the agreements, with no acknowledgment of blood Treaties. It will be shown later that these two different agreement-making methods have had a fundamental impact on the views of the Treaty agreements that eventually influenced the configuration of the Maroon communities.

The blood Treaties presented in the form of oral history raise issues of conflicting claims about autonomy, sovereignty, and self-governance. They are at the root of the challenge to the legality, constitutionality, and authority of the colonial and the post-colonial state, related to African claims to legitimacy versus European claims rooted in written documentation.[13] This is central in exploring Maroons' critical practice of Diaspora and pursuit of sovereignty.

Here we will focus on the written Treaties which, as Werner Zips' *Asafo Warriors* rightly argues, have been privileged in official versions. The written Treaties are a form of documentary practice that has sought to silence oral histories; notably shaped popular understanding of Maroon history, politics, and culture; and significantly affected relations between the Maroons and the state. This is their "instrument effect." They form the almost exclusive basis of the jurisdictional and authorial claims by the colonial and the post-colonial state.

In Appendices I and II are copies of the texts of the two different written Treaties. They detail what the British considered that their agreements with the Maroons entailed. The two written Treaties are not identical but have considerable similarities. The Leeward Maroon Treaty is often considered to have granted slightly greater rights to autonomy than the Windward Maroon Treaty did. The anthropologist Barbara Kopytoff rightly summarizes the similarities and differences between the two written Treaties in the following manner:

> The main points of Cudjoe's [the Leeward Maroons'] treaty were: that the Maroons were recognized as free and were given a grant of land on which they were all to live; that they were to aid in the defense of the island, to hunt down

> other Maroons who did not agree to the same terms, and to return runaways who might in the future fall into their hands; that the Maroon headmen who were to have life tenure, were allowed to administer any punishment but death for crimes whose definition was itself left to the Maroons; that they might sell their produce in the island markets; that white men were to live in the Maroon settlement to facilitate relations with the colonial government [JHA 10, Vol. 3 p. 458]. The treaty signed with Quao [the Windward Maroons] was essentially the same in all these respects. There were, however, several additional clauses that the Governor insisted on before ratification, and one of these organized the Maroon men into companies headed by whites for the purpose of tracking runaway slaves. [14]

Even considering the written Treaties, the British and Maroons have different interpretations. From the British viewpoint, the Treaties were a means of containing rebels, who agreed to become a special class of subjects in the colony of Jamaica.[15] In contrast, the Maroons view the written Treaties as an altered and problematic written version of the blood Treaty agreements. Hence, for the Maroons, the written Treaties were essentially agreements between groups who recognized each other's sovereignty and wished to assist each other.

Over the last two centuries, scholars interpreting and debating the language of the written Treaties have concluded that the Treaties circumscribed Maroons' rights to full sovereignty and autonomous freedom.[16] In *The Iron Thorn*, Carey Robinson argues that the Maroons negotiated Treaties that resulted in agreements that were to their disadvantage because of their lack of experience and literary skills.[17] The anthropologist Barbara Kopytoff considers the Treaties to have weakened Maroons' autonomy, leading to and legitimizing what she refers to as "incomplete polities."[18] In *The Maroons of Jamaica, 1655–1796: A History of Resistance, Collaboration and Betrayal*, Mavis Campbell asserts that the Maroons were inveigled into agreeing to a one-sided treaty in the British favor.[19]

The British made a number of stipulations in the written Treaties that have caused many other scholars to conclude that the Maroons lost their sovereignty. For instance, the Treaties oblige the leader of the Maroons "to wait" on the governor once a year to be informed of duties required of the Maroon communities. They also give the British the right, upon the death of the current chiefs and their listed successors, to appoint new ones. Furthermore, they reserve the right to use capital punishment exclusively for the British colonial government.

However, as Zips points out, the appropriateness of the documentary practice of using the British legal document as the valid interpretation of the Treaties and as a basis for determining the legitimacy of Maroon claims to sovereignty are in question. It is doubtful that the Maroon leaders' native language was English, and that in any case they were literate in it. It is also unlikely that Maroon leaders had much understanding of British law and legal authority. Moreover, the British unilaterally added extra articles to the written Treaties after ending the negotiations with the Maroons.[20]

The Maroons have a different interpretation of the agreements. They reject some but not all of the stipulations of the written documents. They substitute their visions and understandings of the Treaties based on the oral history of oath-taking in the blood rituals.

Whatever the interpretation of the Treaties, there is no doubt that they greatly impacted the subsequent organization of the Maroon communities. In the Maroon view, the Treaties recognized and legitimized their claim of sovereignty over their territorial lands. As Kopytoff argues, the Maroons perceive the Treaties as a part of a sacred charter for the continuing existence of their society.[21] Any attempt to disavow their Treaties was and is seen as a direct threat to the Maroons' collective existence.[22] As Bilby astutely argues, the Treaties are seen by the Maroons as "hallowed covenants that underpin and assure their very existence as separate peoples within the larger society of Jamaica."[23] The signing of the Treaties gave legal recognition to de facto ethnic groups with lands in Jamaica.[24]

The point here is that Maroons contest British claims to sovereignty on documentary grounds. Once again, they use a claim to African connections to substantiate the Maroon worldview. The claim to Africa is based on the notion of pre-colonial independent statist sovereignty that is now transferred to Jamaica and upon which Maroon political organization is based. This is a dispute over what a treaty is. It uses African forms of treaty-making as legitimate and rejects the documentary practice of European treaty-making. The Maroons consider the written Treaties inaccurate partly because they were unilaterally changed after the British and the Maroon leaders made their agreement. The Maroons have remained firm on what they believe the agreement was between the British and themselves.

Moreover, as Rowe-Edwards argues, the blood Treaty in oral history recognizes the Maroons' right to govern themselves, select a leader, create their laws, and secure their territories.[25] The Accompong Maroons see their Treaty with the British as a blood Treaty that is both similar to and different from the widely published and unilaterally amended written Treaty.[26] According to former Deputy Colonel Rowe-Edwards' report about her father in reference to the blood Treaty:

> He said that they [British and Maroons] mixed the blood from their wounds and drank the mixture. . . . Kojo and the white man each, then drank from the mixed

blood. Samuel [Norma Rowe-Edwards's father] said that blood is important and meant that the Treaty was now good.[27]

This statement is vital in its assertion of African forms of treaty-making as valid: an affirmation of African legitimacy. Rowe-Edwards even asserts that "The Treaty is a Blood Treaty," and Kojo "was willing to cut his wrist to draw blood and wanted the white man to do the same."[28]

Similarly, Carey argues that "oral tradition of the Accompong Maroons states that the terms, having been finally agreed, [were] cemented in traditional Maroon fashion, by the mixing of the blood of both black and white in a calabash bowl and drinking of this mixture with rum. This was a blood pact and was taken extremely seriously by the Maroon people."[29] This oral tradition makes claims to the legitimacy of African forms in international relations.

Furthermore, according to Milton McFarlane of the Moore Town Maroons in *Cudjoe of Jamaica*, as he heard from his grandfather:

> Cudjoe [Kojo] was not even aware that [British] Colonel Guthrie would commit the treaty agreements to paper. After both men came to an understanding of the obligations on each side, General Cudjoe [Kojo] considered negotiations ended, congratulated Colonel Guthrie, and was about to leave the meeting place. Guthrie was temporarily baffled by the General's attitude and earnestly asked him to wait until the articles of the agreement were all written down and signed. In turn, the General could not understand why the agreement needed to be recorded; and he said so to Guthrie, emphasising the capability of the Maroons to abide by the treaty just the way it was. In fact, Cudjoe [Kojo] took the opportunity to enlighten Guthrie just a little about Maroons' obedience to their laws over many centuries without having had the necessity to write them on paper—proof that it was enough just to have them know the treaty. And most assuredly the Maroons would be adequately informed.[30]

For the present-day Maroons, the Treaties' essence was to acknowledge the Maroons as a sovereign nation, with the nations giving each other mutual assistance. Maroons usually discuss the essence of the blood Treaties, but not often their specifics. Mann O. Rowe, former Secretary of State of Accompong Town, holds the view that the Treaty stipulates that if any foreign enemies should invade the island, the Maroons are required to help; and on the other hand, if foreign enemies should invade the Maroon community, the British government would help.[31] In addition, former Colonel Harris Cawley (1984–88) asserts that if each side has a problem governing, the other government is required to help the other resolve the matter.[32] Hansley Reid, Chief Abeng Blower of Accompong Town, argues that if there was ever a time when the

Maroons had problems in governing, they could call on the British government to assist them; likewise, if the British government wanted help from the Maroons, it could call on them.[33] From the Maroons' perspective, the support they gave and received from the British and the Government of Jamaica does not nullify their independence.

The written Treaties have about fifteen articles, a number of which the Maroons have alternative interpretations for or else flatly refuse to accept.[34] According to former Colonel Cawley (1984–1988), the written Treaty is one-sided in favor of the British.[35] Carey argues that the "Maroons believe that the terms [in the written Treaty] were altered, dramatically and fundamentally so, and to their detriment."[36] In other words, the Treaty was violated by the British. Carey believes that the British government used "their legislative procedures, to which the Maroons had unwisely declared their loyalty, to break the blood treaty, [and] to use subsequent legislation, passed unilaterally, to tie [up] the Maroons."[37] Carey further asserts that the Maroons have rejected many of the terms of the written Treaties for generations.[38]

There are three articles the Maroons have fundamentally disagreed with or had an alternative interpretation of. In this section, we will focus on the Leeward Maroon Treaty. First, most Maroons dispute that Kojo agreed to only 1,500 acres of land, as indicated in article three of this Treaty (this will be explored further later in the chapter).[39] Second, the Maroons have a different interpretation of the placing of white liaison officers or superintendents in their communities, as stipulated in article fourteen. As Carey observes, the Maroons do not interpret this article as an attempt to control Maroon communities. Rather, the Maroons view the superintendents as commonly placed in the compromising position of renting from and depending on the Maroons. Hence, they often operated in the interests of the Maroons, who contributed to and developed a harmonious relationship with the British authorities.[40] Third and last, as indicated in article fifteen, the Maroons disagree with the British governor or the commander-in-chief having the power to appoint Maroon communities' leaders after the then-current succession of leaders had passed away. Carey believes that it might not have even been a term discussed when Kojo made the treaty agreement.[41]

The point is that the Maroons had a different understanding of their agreement with the British. Maroons' assertions of sovereignty led them to interpret relations with the British in ways that contradicted colonial understanding even against the practical implications and effect of constrictions and limitations on their de facto sovereignty. The fact that they were not seen as "really" free and sovereign did not deter Maroons from representing their condition as sovereign.

Maroon Sovereign Space

Articulation about sovereignty is most significant in Accompong Town out of the four Maroon communities. According to former Colonel Martin-Luther Wright (1967–1984 and 1988–1993) of Accompong, the people there "make up a nation within a nation of the island of Jamaica."[42] In an oral interview, former Colonel Harris Cawley (1984–1988) argues that "the Accompong state" has been recognized as an "independent and sovereign state" since 1738.[43] The former Deputy Colonel Norma Rowe-Edwards affirms that the "Accompong state" is still a sovereign nation on the island of Jamaica.[44] Deputy Colonel Currie argues that Maroons "are a self-governing state, an entity that makes its own laws and lives by its own code of conduct and rules."[45]

Most Accompong Maroons believe they have been an independent nation for centuries. British archival documents going as far back as the 1840s show that Accompong Maroons have been claiming that they are a nation living in a nation since then, at least.[46] In 1980, in a *Jamaica Gleaner* article titled "Maroons Fear Threat to Independence," Maroon leaders assert "that the 1738 treaty signed was still binding" and the "treaty was signed by the blood of our forefathers and if it means death, we shall die, but this treaty must stand."[47] In this sense, their claims to acknowledged independence refer back to the original Treaty. In 1983, in a *Jamaica Gleaner* article, the former Colonel Harris Cawley of Accompong Town argues that the British:

> should not have left the island without acknowledging our [Maroons'] presence; turning over the said island of Jamaica in the hands of their Negro slaves concluding a Constitution without prior consultation with the Maroons with whom they had signed a Peace Treaty in 1738–39. The Constitution that was drawn up by the British for Jamaica should be a Federal Documentation participated in by the said Maroon sovereign state. The Accompong Maroons' Military Parliament has disapproved [of] the manner in which the British had handled the Constitution, and hereby we are requiring the British to make immediate amendment on this important issue.[48]

The fundamental point here is that Accompong Maroons see themselves as sovereign.[49]

The political systems of the various Jamaican Maroon communities are similar in organization. In theory, the colonel holds a position of authority in the administrative, legislative, and judicial matters of his or her community, with minor innovations over the years (see Appendix III for the list of the various colonels/chiefs of the Maroon communities).[50] The colonels choose their council and organize a set of officials and committees. The designations of these officials and committees and their function differ from one Maroon community to another.[51]

In the early days, colonels were generally elected for life, and on the death of the colonel, the current administration would select the next colonel.[52] McFarlane indicates that there was "no specified term of office for a Maroon leader: he may serve for life, or until he himself chooses to surrender his position, although at any time the people may call for an election to choose a new leader."[53] In the late nineteenth century and the early part of the twentieth, as still done in the other three Maroon communities, the colonels were elected for life but with a larger percentage of the population participating.[54]

In principle, the colonels' functions and duties have remained relatively consistent from the time of Jamaican independence. In 1964, the former Colonel Walter Robertson of Accompong (c. 1943–1949 and c. 1957–1967) stated:

> The duties of the colonel are to see that things are in order, mediate in disputes, and preside over meetings of the select councillory [sic] or elders in the village. He also judges and passes sentence in Maroon trials, assisted in the more difficult cases by a kind of jury consisting of four or eight men . . . there were no stealing or wounding offences, but he had to settle a good number of disputes over land boundaries or right of occupancy. Punishment consists most[ly] of fines, as there are no jails in the village.[55]

In *The Sound of the Abeng* (1984), the governing system of Accompong Town is described by the former Colonel Harris Cawley (1984–1988) in the following way:

> During his term of office, the colonel acts as judge, councillor and leader of the people. In his capacity as judicator, the colonel settles land disputes and truces, [as well as] court cases among his people. As councillor he attends public meetings, special functions and private sessions with his council. As leader he represents the people both at home and elsewhere in Jamaica. It is the colonel's responsibility along with his councillors to see that law and order is maintained, that the people are given fair trial, and that plans are made for the development of the community. The colonel is at the head and acts as the leader in all government business.[56]

Prior to Jamaica's independence, the colonel of Accompong Town had been elected on the basis of universal adult suffrage.[57] There was an election about every five years using a ballot box (unlike the three other communities). From the 1950s to the present time, the Accompong Maroons have had special arrangements with the Electoral Office of the Government of Jamaica, which has provided electoral services on counting ballots and assisting with the conduct of the elections.[58] During this period, any Maroons who have been unable to cast ballots in Accompong Town could do so in Kingston, two locations in the parish of St. James (in the city of Montego Bay and community of Garlands), and five in the parish of St. Elizabeth (the communities of Aberdeen, Cedar Spring, Elderslie, Whitehall, and Windsor).[59]

The main representative body of all Maroons is the Maroon Council. In post-colonial Jamaica, the shape of the governing council and its number of members vary from one colonel's tenure to another.[60] In many ways, it currently resembles a combination of an "African traditional system" and a "European parliamentary governing system." The officials tend to number between a dozen and about thirty members, with different governmental divisions, committees, and sub-committees.[61] Just about every Maroon administration has had a deputy colonel, who is second in command and acts in the colonel's absence.[62] The gender ratio of the officials tends to lean heavily in favor of males, but increasingly women are playing direct leadership roles, particularly in Accompong Town and Charles Town.

In the twentieth century, there were a few attempts by Maroons to adopt a constitution. In 1998, a constitution was drafted but not adopted under former Colonel Meredith Rowe's administration of Accompong (1993–1998). In 2004, both local and influential overseas members of the Accompong community submitted another draft for adoption into law. The constitution, which does not seem to have been fully implemented yet, refers to the community as the "The Trelawney Town Maroons of the Sovereign State of Accompong."[63] Overall, the constitution is a 14-page document with a preamble and eight articles covering "legislative branch," "crimes and punishments," "land," "elections," "limitation," "assets," "signators," and "governmental signators." One of its main innovations over the previous governing system was the introduction of the legislative body called Full Maroon Council, which is in some ways a check of the colonel's lawmaking powers.[64]

During the same period, a flag was proposed, with two images imprinted on a maroon-colored background. First, there is symbol of a small Jamaican flag in the upper-righthand corner. Then there is an image of a green-colored Abeng that bears the dates 1655–1738/9.[65]

In Accompong Town, the current Colonel Ferron Williams (2009–present) has his Executive Council and works with four other interrelated political bodies. Colonel Williams confirms that he has an Executive Council of fourteen officials, of whom six or seven are women.[66] The titles and the positions seem fluid. Around 2013, the colonel had a secretary (Ann-Marie Hutchinson) and two deputy colonels: Norma Rowe-Edwards (the first woman to hold that post) and a former colonel, Meredith Rowe.[67] The committees or "ministries" are headed by different council members: Ministry of Education (Garfield Rowe), Ministry of Tourism (Elizabeth Rowe), Ministry of Culture

(Mrs. McKenzie-Rowe), Ministry of Development (Mr. Hutchinson), Ministry of Lands (Kenroy Cawley), and Ministry of Finance (Melita Rowe).[68]

The colonel works with a few other governing bodies. Colonel Williams (2009–present) states that the Board of Elders (or Senior Council) has thirteen members, who advise the Colonel and his Executive Council. The Junior Council, which has about eleven members, mostly female, assists the colonel on matters related to the youth of the community.[69] As mentioned earlier, there is the Full Maroon Council, which has thirteen members.[70]

The development of infrastructure varies from community to community, though it is consistently inadequate. The roads to all of the communities are badly paved. Maroon communities continue to depend on the Jamaican government for infrastructure, which compromises their de facto and de jure sovereignty. The issue poses a dilemma for claims of sovereignty.

In Accompong, there are a number of public facilities and services, financed sometimes by the Maroons but mostly by the Jamaican government or nongovernmental organizations. These include a health clinic, three schools (pre-elementary, elementary, and junior high), a post office/agency, a community center, cemeteries, a recreational site, playing fields, a museum, historic sites and landmarks, libraries, and a computer lab.[71]

The Maroon government presides over a relatively fragile economy. In Accompong Town, people are employed in various industries in the small economic sector.[72] The most significant activities are agriculture and commerce (mainly shopkeeping). According to the Social Development Commission (an agency of the Jamaican government), agriculture is one of the major sources of income, with most of the workers (85 percent) farming ground provisions such as yam and dasheen (taro).[73] Most people in Accompong Town are self-employed—70 percent of the labor force, compared with the Jamaican national average of about 26 percent.[74] The employed are mainly farmers, and the few other workers are domestic workers, construction workers, casual laborers, dressmakers, drivers, vendors, educators, shopkeepers, and clerks.[75] Accompong Town has a working population (15–64 years) of 59.7 percent, 19 percent more than the national Jamaican average.[76]

Maroons seek alternative means to be self-sufficient. They are interested in other means of developing their community, as outlets for selling agricultural products are decreasing.[77] In seeking economic viability and development, the Maroon government has worked with several international organizations, such as the USAID, UNESCO, and the European Union, in the last couple of decades.[78] Many community leaders, such as former Colonel Sidney Peddie (1998–2009), Deputy Colonel Melville Currie, and Abeng Blower Hansley Reid, are interested in developing factories.[79] But many of the developmental efforts have focused on the heritage tourism industry. According to former

Colonel Peddie (1998–2009), the developmental goal is to bring tourists "to the experience of local food, folklore, craft and music, bird watching, caving, and swimming activities."[80] The point is to employ community members in a variety of areas, including serving as tour guides, administrators, and maintenance personnel.[81]

In the current administration, Colonel Williams (2009–present) is continuing this line of development. One of his administration's most controversial initiatives has been the development of the Central Solar Reserve Bank of Accompong (CSRB). According to Timothy E. McPherson Jr., the Minister of Finance of Accompong, in an editorial, the CSRB is located in the "Sovereign Maroon State of Accompong" and it "has been structured as one of the most modern and transformative financial institutions in the Caribbean, which is indicative through the issuance of its own currency, called the LUMI."[82] The current Deputy Colonel Currie believes that Maroon currency circulation must come to pass, since Accompong is a sovereign nation. At the Kojo Day celebration of 2020, Colonel Wallace Sterling (1995–present) of Moore Town Maroon community stated that the currency that will be circulating in Maroon communities will be a factor in their development. Although the bank and currency have support from some members in the Maroon communities, other members are skeptical of the initiative. The Jamaican state and the Bank of Jamaica consider the bank and the currency illegal, but McPherson and some other Maroons believe that the communities are free to decide on their internal matters.[83]

The Maroon government uses heritage tourism as one of the major sources of revenue. In Accompong Town and Charles Town, there are near-daily tours of these settlements and their heritage sites for a fee. Many tourists are Jamaicans, especially from the local high schools and universities, but there are many overseas visitors. In 2006, according to former Deputy Colonel Robinson of Accompong, they had "a fair number of local visitors but . . . on average only five overseas visitors come to the property daily."[84] He also said that tourists visiting for a week or two are usually hosted in the homes of community members, who keep the payments.[85] Thousands of people have been attending the annual Kojo Day celebration, which has an entrance fee.[86] In 2002, when there were about 17,000 patrons in attendance, it was estimated that the year's celebrations netted millions in Jamaican currency from gate receipts.[87] In 2005, former Colonel Meredith Rowe (1993–1998) stated that the Accompong Maroon government alone collects millions per year from tourist visits and other sources.[88] In 2012, 2013, 2015, and 2018, the numbers of these visitors correlated with the author's own experience. These visitors, who also purchase products and services, provide revenue to the wider community. Many locals can sell their products. For the most part, outside vendors on Kojo Day have to rent land and space from local Maroons. Many administrators and tour guides are hired, all local Maroons. It is difficult to identify the annual income from heritage tourism in Accompong. Yet whatever the revenues are there, they are much less in the other Maroon communities.

Most importantly, the land has been the locus of the struggle over sovereignty since the beginning. As Colonel Williams (2009–present) of Accompong asserts through a common Maroon adage, the "land is for the born and the unborn."[89] Maroons view the lands as belonging to the entire community: the ancestors (spirits), the born (living members), and the unborn (all descendants). The authority upon which Maroons' claims are made rests with their ancestors. Maroon families and individuals have plots of land that are passed on from one generation to the next.[90] The unoccupied land of Maroon territory is held by the colonel on behalf of the community.

The Maroons believe that the land tenure system and the colonels' role in its administration are derived directly from Africa.[91] Most Maroons attribute the establishment of the land tenure system to their African ancestors. The Moore Town Maroon writer Milton MacFarlane was told by his grandfather, "Cudjoe [Kojo] was taught, and observed, that the land the Maroons occupied belonged to all of them, and its amicable distribution and use must be perpetuated. In short, the old West African code of communal living was transported almost intact to the Jamaican mountains, enabling the Maroons to govern themselves with internal peace, according to the old ways."[92]

The claims to territory and the authority over it are based on African practices against colonial and post-colonial assertions of authority. Maroon sovereignty signifies the civilized humanity of Africans presented in their capacity for organized forms of statehood, with a particular view of land tenure. This is materially grounded in ancestral/communal land ownership: a claim to African civilization and black civilized humanity. The issue is not so much the conditions, terms, and facticity of sovereignty, but its signification.

Over the centuries, the Maroons have had to struggle to continue to have communally owned lands. The land-ownership pattern of Maroons is a challenge to the state and prevailing Western thought on land ownership and distribution arrangements. In many respects, the control over land is the material condition upon which sovereignty claims are based. Hence, the power to tax (or enforce tax regimes) has become one signifying element of sovereign authority. Accompong Town, more successful than the Windward Maroons, has been effective in maintaining communal lands without paying taxes. From the signing of the Treaties in the eighteenth century, the British government tried to force the Maroons to change their land tenure system in order to tax the land. In 1842, a unilateral law was passed in Jamaica that attempted to end all previous laws concerning the Maroons, including the land tenure rights and the Peace Treaties. The so-called Maroons Lands Allotment Act stated that "all Maroon lands as guaranteed by the treaties were revested in the Crown, to be resurveyed and patented to individual Maroons."[93] According to Carey, in 1845, 1847, and 1856 there were further attempts to divide Maroon lands in order to tax them that the Maroons resisted.[94] In the 1860s, according to the Surveyor-General of British Jamaica, addressing the Colonial Secretary's Office as it pertained to the Accompong Maroons' fierce resistance to the breaking of their communally held lands in order to tax them:

> In 1869, I surveyed the outer lines of the Accompong Township; I also ran the lines of a tract of unpatented land adjoining Accompong with a view to dividing the same in lots to be sold to the Maroons at 5/- per acre. The Maroons, however, refused to pay anything for the land or to have it divided in lots; none was therefore sold. They were made to understand that they could only be permitted to occupy the new land after duly purchasing the same and each man's lot was to be held by him in fee separate from the rest of the Township and not in common as formerly, but these terms they positively refused.[95]

What is important here is that Maroons' authority over land is linked to sovereignty. There is no sovereignty without control of territory. This is what a state is: the apparatus and technology that legitimizes exclusive control over people and territory.

The Accompong Maroons continued to oppose attempts to apportion communal lands. There were further incidents between the British government and Accompong Maroons on this matter between 1901 and 1905.[96] In 1905, the Jamaican colonial government, in collaboration with the Presbyterian Church, stated its readiness to double the amount of land for the Accompong Maroons if they would "agree to be treated hereafter as ordinary landowners, subject to taxes, etc."[97] The Accompong Maroons continue until today to refuse to divide their lands, one of the major reasons being the relationship between land and claims to sovereignty.

In keeping with Maroons' claimed African traditional legacy, the land has a special significance in their communities and historical importance to the communities' origin and development. The point is that Maroons have a different relation to land, imbued with the signifying meaning of Africa.

The relationship to the land is spiritual, political, and economical. Overall, for the Maroons, "spiritual" relates to claims to Africanity, "political" relates to claims to sovereignty, and "economic" relates to the conditions of subsistence. As indicated earlier, there are a few major sites of spiritual significance: at least two separate burial sites, sixty Sealed Grounds, and the Kindah Tree.[98] Politically, the land is Maroon sovereign space, and for Accompong, it was the place, an area called Peace Cave, where the Treaty was believed to have been concluded.[99] Economically, there are also many trails throughout western Jamaica, including the important Maroon Trail that is being opened up for eco-tourism, which have the historical significance of being Maroon lands.[100]

The settlements are the stronghold of the sovereignty of the Maroons: the land their ancestors won from the British. The written Treaty acknowledges Maroon ownership of land, but it limits the territorial size to a few thousand acres. The blood Treaty, made through a treaty-signing method embraced as African, is used to argue the true size of the Maroon lands. The Maroon view on the entire lands, whether or not it is acknowledged by the Jamaican state, is a critical practice that contests the prevailing Western political and philosophical understanding of land use. Control of and authority over land use is the material condition of sovereignty. All states make claims to land and the ultimate right to land use, but the difference here is the way in which authority is legitimized and normalized. For the West, it is based on the documentary practice of constitutionality; for the Maroons it is the African-derived practice of the blood Treaty and its associated orality.

The Accompong Maroons claim control over a sizable portion of the western section of the island of Jamaica. It is a critical practice in both utterances and acts that the claim is sustained. At different times and from different people, there are differences in viewpoint regarding the exact size and contour of the lands. The Accompong Maroons, supported by many Maroon elders, claim not only the territorial lands of 1,500 or 3,000 acres of Accompong Town but also a large section of western Jamaica, including an ecologically unique rainforest area with bauxite and limestone deposits called the Cockpit Country, about 200 square miles.[101]

The current colonel of Accompong, Ferron Williams (2009–present) himself holds the view that Maroon territory is much larger than the 1,500 acres presented in the written Treaty. He believes that "the Jamaican government knows that they have taken most of our lands."[102] Colonel Williams understands that a number of areas miles away from Accompong Town are Maroon lands, including Fullerswood, located in the neighboring parish of Westmoreland.[103] Colonel Williams believes that land is power, and the blood Treaty acknowledged the lands as belonging to the Maroons.[104] Colonel Williams remarks that:

> I hope that a [Maroon] regime someday will be as brave and say to the authorities in Jamaica, "We need for you to give us back our lands." In fact, I led a delegation from here to see the Governor-General, who is the head of Jamaica. The Prime Minister is not the head of Jamaica, you know. It is the Governor-General; and we took a map of the Cockpit Country and if we did not own the

> land [of the Cockpit Country as indicated in the Treaty] we would not have been maintaining the roads. Why would you be maintaining roads to Trelawny if you did not have the land leading to Trelawny? Why would you maintain the road going to St. James . . . if the land doesn't belong to you?[105]

At the Kojo Day celebration in 2017, in reference to the Cockpits, Colonel Williams (2009–present) stated in the presence of officials from Jamaica and the UK (the Governor-General in particular) that "these lands that our foreparents sacrificed their lives for are being taken away."[106] The issue here is the legitimacy of the blood Treaty that dictates the territory's true size and location.

According to the former Deputy Colonel of Accompong Norma Rowe-Edwards, before the treaty agreements, the leaders of the Maroons, "Nanny and Kojo, employed a strategy that incorporated the entire expanse of the mountainous Cockpit terrain"—clearly a region they claimed as their own.[107] Rowe-Edwards states that in making the treaty agreement, "Kojo requested all of the lands in the Cockpit Country from seacoast to seacoast."[108]

The former Colonel Harris Cawley (1984–1988) of Accompong affirms that the Maroons were in Jamaica before the British invaded, and they had an earlier stake to the land after the Spanish left. They believe earlier arrival in Jamaica also gives them a temporal claim through prior ownership. For former Colonel Cawley, all of Cockpit Country and beyond are Maroon lands.[109] As former Colonel Harris Cawley asserts in *The Sound of the Abeng* (1984), "many Maroons still refer to this community [of Accompong Town] as Trelawny Town (Cudjoe Town). Accompong was located to the South of Trelawny Town in the areas now known as White Hall, Bethsalem, and Harmony Hall. But these areas have been taken away from the Maroons and settled by the Jamaican government."[110] He believes at least 20 percent of the lands of Jamaica belong to the Maroons.[111] During his administration in the mid-1980s, he was an ardent proponent of the Jamaican government recognizing Maroon lands beyond the mere 1,500 acres.[112]

The Accompong Maroon leaders have been vocal in the local press, mainly the *Jamaica Gleaner*, on the matter of their land rights. The press began giving specific Maroon coverage, starting in the early twentieth century. One of the most vocal Maroon leaders has been former Colonel Meredith Rowe (1993–1998) of Accompong. A *Jamaica Gleaner* article, of August 19, 1997, titled "Maroons Making Strides," states:

> The Accompong Town Maroons in St. Elizabeth are once again accusing the government of trying to steal their ancestral lands. Former Colonel and President of the Maroons Federal House of Assembly Meredith Rowe, speaking at a press conference in Montego Bay on Tuesday, accused the government of sabotage and said that they were not forthright in their discussions on the issuing of Maroon lands for the proposed Cockpit Country Conservation project.[113]

A year later, in 1998, via former Colonel Meredith Rowe (1993–1998), the paper stated that "The Accompong Maroons are claiming that they control 150,000 acres of property and that the cockpits, located in the hills of St. Elizabeth and upper Trelawny, falls within it." [114]

Deputy Colonel Melville Currie of Accompong believes that the treaty agreement between the Maroons and the British in 1738 was an acknowledgment of lands larger than the Cockpit Country, going into the parishes of St. Elizabeth, St. James, Trelawny, and Westmoreland. His understanding is that the Cockpits is referred to as a country because Maroons are the only people and nation that lived in it at that time. He states that the Maroons already had the Cockpit Country before the wars in the seventeenth and eighteenth centuries, and lands were negotiated that were outside of the Cockpit Country.[115]

In 1998, members of the Maroon Advancement Committee (of Accompong), as reported in the *Jamaica Gleaner*, "accused the government of capturing and poaching on Maroon land for which they said they didn't have the resources to legally reestablish their boundaries." A member of the Committee, Hugh Rowe, "was concerned with the gradual advancement of crown land boundaries into the Accompong territory. He said that over the years Accompong had been decreasing in size because of legislation redefining crown land boundaries and the actions of unscrupulous government surveyors."[116]

It is steeped in the Maroons' oral history that they own significant portions of lands in Jamaica. According to Milton McFarlane in *Cudjoe of Jamaica*:

> When the articles [of the Peace Treaty] were agreed upon, the Maroons had controlled, for nearly a hundred years, almost all of the lands in the mountainous regions of Jamaica. And Cudjoe [Kojo] won an agreement that recognized the continued ownership and control of those lands by the Maroons. However, according to Grandpa Wallen, as time passed the Backra [White] government laid claim to most of the territory, and by his day, all the Maroons had left were the five village areas in which they actually lived and cultivated; and so the real borders were a matter of dispute.[117]

In *Maroon Story*, Carey uses oral histories and British archival documents to support the claim of Accompong Maroons having greater territorial claims than 1,500 acres. According to Carey, the Accompong Maroons can still identify those lands, for they know where they touched the sea on the south coast and where they reached the sea on the north coast.[118] She argues that:

> When the first draft of the Treaty went to the Board of Trade and Plantations, the area of land referred to in that draft was 15,000 acres, with those numbers written numerically. The last zero was erased to make the figure 1,500 acres and thereby reduce the acreage by 13,500 acres. On the original documents, a copy

of which the Accompong Town Maroons have in their possession, it is easy to identify the correct acreage.[119]

Furthermore, based on Carey's account, the Accompong Maroons think that it is unlikely that Kojo "who had the run of much of the western countryside around their settlement, would have been so inept as to settle for a mere 1,500 acres."[120] The author believes there was a devious design of patenting land close to Accompong Town. This was the overt encroachment, she believes, by the early eighteenth-century Governor Edward Trelawny, who secretly sought to restrict the lands Kojo possessed to the most mountainous and non-arable sections.[121]

In the last three centuries, Maroons and British have been in a struggle over control of territories in Jamaica. There is no record of recognition of Accompong having more than 1,500 or 3,000 acres of land in the British and Jamaican archives. However, Accompong Maroons have historically believed that they were not given but won a much larger territorial land than they have at present. There are numerous British archival documents and newspaper accounts showing Maroons' consistent struggle over lands in western and eastern Jamaica in the entire post-treaty era, from the eighteenth to the twenty-first century.

The British documented the claims of Maroons to wider territorial lands shortly after the treaty agreements. Land conflict occurred between Accompong and the British government several times, including in 1870, 1880, and 1883.[122] In the 1890s, in the *Jamaica Gleaner*, there was a report of a dispute at Fullerswood Estate (some distance from Accompong Town) because Accompong Maroons claimed that the Salmon family was occupying lands that belonged to them. In the late 1930s and early 1940s, there were further disputes and negotiations on lands between the Maroons and the British government. In 1939, a *Jamaica Standard* newspaper article titled "Governor Offers the Maroons of Accompong Grant of More Lands," Governor Sir Arthur Richards told the Maroons "that he was prepared to grant them the lands which they were claiming from the Government of Jamaica under their two-hundred-year-old treaty with the British government." The article further states that "in addition the Governor said he was proposing to the Maroon leaders a plan for the reservation of two to three thousand acres of the Cockpit Country to be held in trust by the community for the benefit of further generations of Maroons." The British government at least acknowledged and attempted to respond to Maroons' claim for larger pieces of land that surpassed the previously acknowledged 1,500 acres. In the late 1930s, the government did, in fact, offer up to 4,000 additional acres of land, but it came with requirements of taxes that the Maroons rejected.[123]

The Maroons' African view of land highlights the symbolic significance of control over territory. The struggle is to maintain control over territory against the intrusion of the Jamaican state. It is also over the terms of such control: sovereign control or a form of constrained autonomy subject to the exercise of state power.

Environmental Stance

Informed by their own understanding of their African heritage, the Maroons have ideas and visions of harmonious and reciprocal use of environmental space. This critical practice of the Maroons challenges the prevailing state-centric and Western ideologies of man's relationship with the land. It particularly challenges the Lockean idea of land ownership and use. In Jamaica, Maroons claiming sovereign powers over a sizeable portion of Jamaica are ideologically struggling with the state over land use that is informed by African origin and traditional view of land.

The Maroons believe that their community and the surrounding areas, especially the wider Cockpit Country, should be protected and preserved in line with the African ancestral views. The plant and animal life, among the other things from the land, is important in the farming community. According to Rowe-Edwards, they, as Maroons, have historically truly lived "in harmony with the environment; each one was a successful practicing environmentalist."[124] She elaborates that the Maroons were the first people and community in Jamaica to practice sustainable forestry. They believe in planting a tree for every tree removed.[125] In her view, "Man and environment were engaged in an interaction where each harmoniously cared for each other."[126] This was said with the belief that the view came from her African ancestors.

Of course, this view also reflects Maroons' position and alignment with the global environmentalist movement, from which they receive active support internationally. It is also consistent with the demands of eco-tourism, from which the Maroons derive revenues. The claim to African tradition justifies these strategic and economic alliances.

In the Maroon communities, plants and herbs, including the rich diversity of the Cockpit Country, have been historically treasured, and their protection is seen as a continuation of African traditions. Plants and herbs are used for healthcare, from treating the common cold to caring for the mentally disturbed. According to Rowe-Edwards, a nurse by profession, the tradition of herbal medicine was practiced by her African ancestors and passed on from one generation to the next.[127] Accompong Maroon Council member and secretary Ann-Marie Hutchinson said that herbal plants were widely used but have declined in recent years.[128] The Junior Council of the Williams Administration was involved in attempts to revive herbal use in the community and educate the younger children about the environmental significance of the community's vegetation.[129] Deputy Colonel Melville Currie considers the herbs and plants in the Cockpit Country very important and believes that cures for AIDS and cancer could be found in the area.[130] Fundamentally, all of this belief is tied to continued African traditions and relates to enunciations of Africa. It is also a critical practice of struggle against the state to conduct African traditions in a sovereign space.

The Accompong Maroons, seeing themselves in line with traditional African views, agree with each other on the protection and preservation of their community, which includes the wider Cockpit Country.[131] It is a critical practice of living African traditions in their own territory. At the turn of the twenty-first century, the Maroons were up in arms against further bauxite mining in the Cockpit Country, which they understand harms the environment. According to a *Jamaica Gleaner* article, the Maroons are calling on Jamaicans to join in the discussion, as they are ready to "go to war" with the Government of Jamaica over the matter.[132] Council Member Hutchinson of Accompong said she is in total agreement with the opposition to bauxite mining in the Cockpits.[133] The community wants its peace and does not want to be disturbed, so they are firmly against the idea of bringing machines to destroy "our habitat."[134]

Other Maroons joined the struggle to save the Cockpits from harm, to protect this presumed African way of life. In a *Jamaica Gleaner* headline article of June 8, 2007, titled "Int[ernationa]l Maroons defend Cockpit," the Overseas Maroon Council came out against bauxite mining.

> "We are unrepentantly opposed to the mining of the Cockpit Country. This section of the world should be protected because of its history," said President Carol Barnett on Saturday. Adding that the Cockpit Country is not just for the Maroons, but also for Jamaicans in general, Ms. Barnett, an Accompong Maroon living in the United States, pledged the backing of all 10 chapters of the council—spanning the United States, the United Kingdom and the Caribbean—as well as the Suriname Maroons in the fight for the cause.

Then the leaders of the other three Maroon communities—Charles Town (Colonel Frank Lumsden), Moore Town (Colonel Wallace Sterling), and Scot's Hall (Colonel Noel Prehay)—all committed to stopping mining in the Cockpit Country.[135]

When there was subsequent renewed interest in mining in the Cockpit Country, Maroons once again opposed it. In 2016, at the Kojo Day celebration, Maroon leaders vowed to protect their ancestral homeland, with a renewed discussion of the rich bauxite deposit in the Cockpit Country. Colonel Williams (2009–present) insisted that the Maroons will do what it takes to protect the lands they own.[136] In 2017, Maroons played a role in banning mining in designated areas of the Cockpit Country.[137] In 2019, the Council of Overseas Maroons along with other Jamaicans staged a demonstration at the United Nations in New York, coinciding with Jamaican Prime Minister Andrew Holness's trip to address the UN on climate change, to register their opposition to mining activities in Cockpit Country.[138] Although this struggle over land use is part of the global counter-hegemonic and anti-systemic formations, for the Maroons the struggle is partially rooted in the ability to continue African traditions in their sovereign territory.

Conclusion

The use of the African Diaspora by Jamaican Maroon communities supports and gives language to claims of sovereignty. Links to origins in ancient African civilizations are used to explain the continuation of sovereignty of the Maroons in Jamaica. The Maroons further base their claim to sovereignty from an African perspective on the international treaty agreements with the British that they consider binding. Hence, Maroons have endeavored to implement their vision of the Maroon state in harmonious and reciprocal relations with their environmental space and territory. This very aspiration inserts Maroons into the articulated space of the African Diaspora. In examining Maroons' claims to sovereignty, what is at play is Diaspora, challenging abjection and positioning shared origin and consciousness.

Notes

1. Harris Cawley, interview by author, Accompong Town, St. Elizabeth, Jamaica, August 1, 2012.
2. Bev Carey, *The Maroon Story: The Authentic and Original History of the Maroons in the History of Jamaica, 1490–1880* (Gordon Town, Jamaica: Agouti Press, 1997), 148, 334, 366.
3. Milton C. McFarlane, *Cudjoe of Jamaica: Pioneer for Black Freedom in the New World* (Short Hills, NJ: R. Enslow, 1977), 84.
4. Wallace Sterling, interview by author, Moore Town, Portland, Jamaica, December 1, 2011.
5. Frank Lumsden, interview by author, Charles Town, Portland, Jamaica, December 6, 2011.

6. Noel Prehay, "Welcome Remarks," (speech, Quao Day celebration, Charles Town, Jamaica, June 23, 2011).

7. Melville Currie, interview by author, Accompong Town, St. Elizabeth, Jamaica, August 14, 2012.

8. Ibid.

9. Norma Rowe-Edwards, *My Father Said: A Story about the Accompong Maroons 1655–1738* (Riviera Beach, FL: Emerge Publishing Group, 2011), 123.

10. Prehay, "Introductory Remarks."

11. Mann O. Rowe, interview by an unknown interviewer, undated, interview T265, African Caribbean Institute of Jamaica, Kingston, Jamaica.

12. Colonel Martin-Luther Wright, "Accompong Maroons of Jamaica," in *Maroon Heritage Archaeological, Ethnographic, and Historical Perspectives*, ed. E. Kofi Agorsah (Barbados: Canoe Press, 1994), 64.

13. Werner Zips, *Nanny's Asafo Warriors: The Jamaican Maroons' African Experience* (Kingston: Ian Randle, 2011), 195–197.

14. Barbara Klamon Kopytoff, "Jamaican Maroon Political Organization: The Effects of the Treaties," *Social and Economic Studies* 25, no. 2 (1976): 90.

15. Barbara Klamon Kopytoff, "Colonial Treaty as Sacred Charter of the Jamaican Maroons," *Ethnohistory* 26, no. 1 (1979): 46.

16. The following are a few texts that explore the written Treaties in great detail: Edward Long's *The History of Jamaica, or, General Survey of the Antient and Modern State of That Island With Reflections on Its Situation Settlements, Inhabitants, Climate, Products, Commerce, Laws, and Government* (1774); Bryan Edwards and William Young's *An Historical Survey of the Island of Saint Domingo Together with an Account of the Maroon Negroes in the Island of Jamaica, and a History of the War in the West Indies, in 1793, and 1794* (1801); Robert Charles Dallas's *The History of the Maroons* (1803); Barbara Kopytoff's "Jamaican Maroon Political Organization: The Effects of the Treaties" (1976) and "Colonial Treaty: As Sacred Charter of the Jamaican Maroons" (1979); Milton McFarlane's *Cudjoe of Jamaica: Pioneer for Black Freedom in the New World* (1977); Kenneth Bilby's "Swearing by the Past, Swearing to the Future: Sacred Oaths, Alliances, and Treaties Among the Guianese and Jamaican Maroons" (1997); and Bev Carey's *The Maroon Story: The Authentic and Original History of the Maroons in the History of Jamaica, 1490–1880* (1997).

17. Carey Robinson, *The Iron Thorn: The Defeat of the British by the Jamaican Maroons* (Kingston: Kingston Publishers, 1993), 120–121.

18. Barbara Klamon Kopytoff, "The Maroons of Jamaica: An Ethnohistorical Study of Incomplete Polities, 1655–1905" (PhD diss., University of Pennsylvania, 1973).

19. Mavis Christine Campbell, *The Maroons of Jamaica: 1655–1796* (Trenton, NJ: Africa World Press, 1990), 129.

20. Ibid., 141.

21. Kopytoff, "Colonial Treaty," 70.

22. Ibid., 46.

23. Kenneth Bilby, "Swearing by the Past, Swearing to the Future: Sacred Oaths, Alliances, and Treaties Among the Guianese and Jamaican Maroons," *Ethnohistory: The Bulletin of the Ohio Valley Historic Indian Conference* 44, no. 4 (1997): 656.

24. Kenneth M. Bilby, "Maroon Autonomy in Jamaica," *Cultural Survival Quarterly* 25, no. 4 (2002), 2–3.

25. Rowe-Edwards, *My Father Said*, 123.

26. Currie, interview; Cawley, interview; McFarlane, *Cudjoe of Jamaica*, 16.

27. Rowe-Edwards, *My Father Said*, 113.

28. Ibid., 112.

29. Carey, *Maroon Story*, 331.

30. McFarlane, *Cudjoe of Jamaica*, 129–130.

31. Mann O. Rowe, interview.

32. Cawley, interview.

33. Hansley Reid, interview by author, Accompong Town, St. Elizabeth, Jamaica, December 21, 2011.

34. Carey, *Maroon Story*, 364, 365, 366.

35. Cawley, interview.

36. Carey, *Maroon Story*, 336.

37. Ibid., 338.

38. Ibid., 340.

39. Ibid., 359.

40. Ibid., 365.

41. Ibid.

42. Wright, "Accompong Maroons of Jamaica," 67.

43. Cawley, interview.

44. Rowe-Edwards, *My Father Said*, 11.

45. "Maroons Accuse Govt. of Land Capturing and Culture Damage," *Jamaica Gleaner* (Kingston), January 8, 1988.

46. Kopytoff, "Colonial Treaty," 55.

47. "Maroons Fear Threat to Independence," *Jamaica Gleaner* (Kingston), September 29, 1980.

48. "Opinions," *Jamaica Gleaner* (Kingston), December 3, 1983.

49. It is doubtful that Cawley used the phrase "Negro slaves" but this is how it was published in the *Jamaica Gleaner*.

50. Werner Zips, "Laws in Competition," *The Journal of Legal Pluralism and Unofficial Law* 28, no. 37–38 (1996): 291.

51. Currie, interview; Kathleen Wilson, "The Performance of Freedom: Maroons and the Colonial Order in Eighteenth-Century Jamaica and the Atlantic Sound," *The William and Mary Quarterly* 66, no. 1 (2009): 72.

52. Wright, "Accompong Maroons of Jamaica," 68.

53. McFarlane, *Cudjoe of Jamaica*, 26–27.

54. Wright, "Accompong Maroons of Jamaica," 68; Rowe-Edwards, *My Father Said*, 124.

55. "Accompong Maroons at odds over election of colonel," *Daily Gleaner* (Kingston), July 19, 1967, 26; "Maroons at Accompong," *Jamaica Gleaner* (Kingston), March 21, 1964.

56. Harris N. Cawley, *The Sound of the Abeng: A Short Synopsis on the Accompong Maroons* (Accompong Town: Speedy Prints, 1986), 11–12.

57. “Maroon Col. Thomas James Cawley Dies”; “Ex-Colonel of Maroons dies at 100,” *Jamaica Gleaner* (Kingston), August 5, 1971.

58. “Walker, “Rowe at Odds over Maroon Polls,” *Jamaica Gleaner* (Kingston), November 19, 1998.

59. “Maroons Identify Voting Sites,” *Jamaica Gleaner* (Kingston), November 22, 1998; Ferron Williams, interview by author, Accompong Town, St. Elizabeth, Jamaica, January 7, 2012.

60. Cawley, *The Sound of the Abeng*, 12.

61. Ibid.; Wright, “Accompong Maroons of Jamaica,” 68.

62. Cawley, *Sound of the Abeng*, 10.

63. The Trelawney Town Maroons of the Sovereign State of Accompong Constitution.

64. Ibid.

65. Accompong Town Maroon Community, “Sovereign State of Accompong Maroons,” accessed May 29, 2020, https://www.accompong-gov.org/.

66. Garfield Rowe, interview by author, Accompong Town, St. Elizabeth, Jamaica, January 10, 2013; Ann-Marie Hutchinson, interview by author, Accompong Town, St. Elizabeth, Jamaica, December 28, 2011.

67. Williams, interview.

68. Williams, interview; Garfield Rowe, interview; Hutchinson, interview.

69. Williams, interview; Hutchinson, interview.

70. Williams, interview; Currie, interview.

71. Social Development Commission (SDC). *Community Profile: Accompong* (Kingston, Jamaica: SDC Research Department, 2011), 45.

72. Ibid., 52.

73. Ibid., 4–5.

74. Ibid., 4–5, 48.

75. Ibid., 4–5.

76. Ibid., 17.

77. Melvin Harris, “Maroon Foundation set for Accompong,” *Jamaica Gleaner* (Kingston), January 6, 2005, accessed December 2, 2012, http://jamaica-gleaner.com/gleaner/20050106/western/western4.html; “The Maroon Challenge—Peddie to Tackle Roads, Water and Unemployment,” *Jamaica Gleaner* (Kingston), June 10, 2004, accessed December 3, 2012, http://jamaica-gleaner.com/gleaner/20040610/cornwall/cornwall4.html; Roy Sanford, “Traditional Rules!” *Jamaica Gleaner* (Kingston), January 13, 2010.

78. Yvonne Chin, “The Herb Women of Accompong,” *Jamaica Gleaner* (Kingston), November 4, 2002; “Accompong Maroons Cry Foul,” *Jamaica Gleaner* (Kingston), June 29, 2000; Garfield Rowe, interview; “UNESCO trains 30 Volunteers for Accompong Maroon Radio Station,” *Jamaica Observer* (Kingston), February 12, 2019, accessed March 27, 2020, http://www.jamaicaobserver.com/latestnews/UNESCO_trains_30_volunteers_for_Accompong_Maroon_radio_station?profile=1470.

79. “The Maroon Challenge,” *Jamaica Gleaner* (Kingston), June 10, 2010; Currie, interview.

80. "Accompong Maroons Creating Tourism Product," *Jamaica Gleaner* (Kingston), August 10, 2008.

81. Ibid.

82. Timothy E. McPherson Jr., "BOJ has no Sway Over Maroon Bank," *Jamaica Gleaner* (Kingston), May 7, 2018, accessed March 25, 2020, http://jamaica-gleaner.com/article/letters/20180507/letter-day-boj-has-no-sway-over-Maroon-bank.

83. "Lumi Still on Track, Says Maroon Chief," *Jamaica Observer* (Kingston), January 12, 2020, accessed March 27, 2020, http://www.jamaicaobserver.com/news/lumi-still-on-track-says-Maroon-chief-time-has-come-for-economic-freedom-argues-colonel-wallace-sterling_184347.

84. Claudia Gardner, "Maroons not Capitalising on Tourism," *Jamaica Gleaner* (Kingston), January 11, 2006.

85. Ibid.

86. Horace Hines, "Suriname, Ghana Maroon Groups for Accompong Celebrations," *Jamaica Observer* (Kingston) January 3, 2008, accessed December 4, 2012, http://www.jamaicaobserver.com/pfversion/130968_Suriname--Ghana-Maroon-groups-for-Accompong-celebrations-Sunday.

87. Conroy Walker, "Accompong Celebrations a Success Despite Concerns about Event Date," *Jamaica Observer* (Kingston), January 12, 2002, accessed January 25, 2014, http://www.jamaicaobserver.com/pfversion/19578_Accompong-celebrations-a-success-despite-concerns-about-event-date.

88. "Accompong Maroons at Odds Over Land," *Jamaica Observer* (Kingston), December 24, 2005, accessed December 4, 2012, http://www.jamaicaobserver.com/pfversion/95214_Accompong-Maroons-at-odds-over-land.

89. Williams, interview.

90. Ibid.

91. Wright, "Accompong Maroons of Jamaica," 15.

92. McFarlane, *Cudjoe of Jamaica*, 26.

93. Werner Zips, "'We Are Landowners' Territorial Autonomy and Land Tenure in the Jamaican Maroon Community of Accompong," *Journal of Legal Pluralism and Unofficial Law* 30, no. 40 (1998): 109.

94. Carey, *Maroon Story*, 559.

95. "T.H. to Colonial Office," October 20, 1882, Box 1/5/76/3/23, Colonial Secretary's Office, Jamaica Archives and Record Department, Spanish Town, Jamaica.

96. Smith, "Stakeholder Involvement in the Decision-Making," 57.

97. "Status of Maroons," *Jamaica Gleaner* (Kingston), September 30, 1905.

98. "Spirit Possession in Afro-Jamaican Religions and the Kromanti Play," African Caribbean Institute/Jamaica Memory Bank, accessed March 12, 2013, http://acij-ioj.org.jm/spirit-possession-in-afro-jamaican-religions-and-the-kromanti-play/; DjeDje, "Remembering Kojo," 95.

99. Currie, interview.

100. Hutchinson, interview.

101. Cawley, interview; Reid, interview; James Chambers, interview by the author, Accompong Town, St. Elizabeth, Jamaica, December 22, 2011; Mann O. Rowe, interview.

102. Williams, interview.
103. Ibid.
104. Ibid.
105. Ibid.
106. "Accompong Maroon Chief Vows to Protect Cockpit Country," *Jamaica Observer* (Kingston), January 08, 2017, accessed March 26, 2020, http://www.jamaicaobserver.com/news/Accompong-Maroon-chief-vows-to-protect-Cockpit-Country.
107. Rowe-Edwards, *My Father Said*, 83.
108. Ibid., 113.
109. Cawley, interview.
110. Cawley, *Sound of the Abeng*, 10.
111. Cawley, interview.
112. "Opinions."
113. Wright, "Accompong Maroons Cry Foul."
114. "Maroons Accuse Govt. of Land Capturing."
115. Currie, interview.
116. Ibid.
117. McFarlane, *Cudjoe of Jamaica*, 129.
118. Carey, *Maroon Story*, 38.
119. Ibid., 337, 338, 359.
120. Ibid., 359.
121. Ibid., 420.
122. Daniel Lee Schafer, "The Maroons of Jamaica: African Slave Rebels in the Caribbean" (PhD diss., University of Minnesota, 1974), 174.
123. "Governor Offers the Maroons."
124. Rowe-Edwards, *My Father Said*, 102.
125. Ibid., 120.
126. Ibid., 72.
127. Rowe-Edwards, *My Father Said*, 72.
128. Ikamellia Foster, interview by author, Accompong Town, St. Elizabeth, Jamaica, December 30, 2011; Hutchinson, interview.
129. Hutchinson, interview.
130. Currie, interview.
131. Garfield Rowe, interview; Foster, interview; Currie, interview; Cawley, interview.
132. Claudine Housen, "Carib Judged to Aid Maroons in Cockpit Resistance," *Jamaica Gleaner* (Kingston), January 13, 2007.
133. Hutchinson, interview.
134. Ibid.
135. Claudine Housen, "Int'l Maroons Defend Cockpit," *Jamaica Gleaner* (Kingston), June 8, 2007.
136. Garfield Myers, "Accompong Maroons Reaffirm Claim to Cockpit Country," *Jamaica Observer* (Kingston), January 07, 2016, accessed March 26, 2020, http://www.jamaicaobserver.com/news/Accompong-Maroons-reaffirm-claim-to-Cockpit-Country_48072.

137. Robert J. Connell, "Maroon Ecology: Land, Sovereignty, and Environmental Justice," *The Journal of Latin American and Caribbean Anthropology* 25, no. 2 (June 2019): 231.

138. "Jamaicans Stage Cockpit Country Protest Outside UN HQ," *Jamaica Gleaner* (Kingston), September 28, 2019, accessed March 25, 2020, http://jamaica-gleaner.com/article/lead-stories/20190928/jcans-stage-cockpit-country-protest-outside-un-hq.

Conclusion

> The food we cook, the dancing that we have, the drum we play are all part of the African Diaspora and African system.
>
> —Deputy Colonel Melville Currie of Accompong Town Maroon Community[1]

DIFFERENT COMMUNITIES OF AFRICAN descent engage the concept of the African Diaspora in distinctive ways. How these communities engage the African Diaspora and its core components—abjection, origin, and shared consciousness—informs their means of emancipatory politics toward the ultimate goal of total recognition of the full humanity of peoples of African descent. These means are articulated and critically practiced, varying over time, place, and space. As an analytical device, the African Diaspora reveals how Jamaican Maroons uniquely seek to improve black standing, notably through claims that enhance the assertion of sovereignty.

The African Diaspora is the network produced out of mutually recognized enunciations of blackness that create global linkages among all peoples with claims to origin in Africa and who challenge black abjection. Therefore, I have explored how diasporic articulations can be involved in critical practice. When Diaspora is articulated as a critical practice, it is ultimately engaged in the struggle for black freedom, sovereignty, and self-determination. *The Workings of Diaspora* is a case study of Jamaican Maroons (highlighting Accompong) and their critical practice, articulation, and politics of the African Diaspora.

Maroon sovereignty can be seen as an instance of the critical practice and articulation of the African Diaspora. Sovereignty is an assertion of black humanity. It is based on claims to African history and authenticity that are enunciated locally yet link Maroons to black people everywhere. Their local specificity is the direct relationship claimed to authentic African forms. The political, economic, and social organization of Maroons differ from other communities of African descent. The enunciations of blackness differ significantly, even though these communities make mutually recognized claims to blackness, and it is on the basis of such recognition that linkages are made among them.

Sovereignty is a critical practice of Maroons. Thus, Maroons seek to have the Jamaican state fully recognize their sovereignty. For instance, in the 1970s, Colonel C. L. G. Harris (1964–1995), as a senator in the Jamaican national government, attempted to have the Jamaican state recognize Maroons' autonomy, though unsuccessfully.[2] In a 2011 *Jamaica Gleaner* newspaper article, Colonel Williams (2009–present) called for Maroon communities' sovereignty to be recognized in the Jamaican Constitution.[3] In the annual Kojo Day celebrations of 2013, 2015, and 2018, the author heard Maroon leaders calling on the Jamaican state and the British government to fully recognize their sovereignty. Most recently, at the Kojo Day celebration in 2020, Colonel Rodolph Pink (2016–present) of Scot's Hall Maroon community said that the Maroons are sovereign and called for the post-colonial Jamaican state to ratify the Treaties.[4]

However, the Jamaican government does not fully recognize Maroon sovereignty, although it uses Maroon history in creating the narrative of Jamaican nationhood. Many government officials express solidarity with Maroons as foundational to Jamaican national independence. For instance, in 2009, at Accompong Town's annual Kojo Day celebration, the State Minister for Mining and Telecommunications, Lawrence Broderick, stated:

> There are certain defining moments in every nation's history that helped to create the current atmosphere that everyone enjoys. And that peace treaty which was signed in 1738 represents a fighting spirit of our people to take on the odds at all times. If there was no Captain Cudjoe [Kojo], there would have been no Marcus Garvey, Malcolm X, Barack Obama or Usain Bolt, so we must celebrate and remind everyone that we can triumph in any situation.[5]

Moreover, in 2012, at Accompong Town, the annual Kojo Day celebration was made the first official event of Jamaica's 50th anniversary of independence. Sydney Bartley, Principal Director of Culture in the Ministry of Youth and Culture of the Jamaican Government, asserted that if it had not been for the struggle of Kojo and Nanny, they would not be celebrating today but perhaps would still be "somewhere cutting cane."[6] Then in 2013, at Accompong Town, Lisa Hanna, Minister of Youth and Culture, connecting with Maroons, argued for Jamaicans to return to their roots in order to move forward, and observed that they could learn a lot from the Asante governance structure, which ensured that every member of the community was taken care of.[7] She later declared that she aims to engage the Maroon community in a cultural mission for the protection of Jamaica's children, recapturing the Asante approach of working with the community to care for, respect, and love their children.[8]

The post-colonial Jamaican state embraces the narrative of Maroons as being freedom fighters and forerunners of Jamaican nationhood—in this nationhood that Maroons are part of but not sovereign from. Since the 1970s, Nanny of the Maroons has been one of the national heroes of Jamaica, and few national events pass without acknowledgment of Maroons' contribution to nationhood. This is especially true for Emancipation Day, Heroes' Day, and Independence Day. Government officials have increasingly visited the various Maroon communities and explored plans of cooperation with them.

Maroon communities are entangled with a variety of apparatuses of the Jamaican state, including educational institutions (such as the University of Technology), cultural centers or institutes (including the Institute of Jamaica, the Jamaica National Heritage Trust, and the Jamaica Cultural Development Commission), environmental centers (such as the Environmental Foundation of Jamaica), and community-development offices (including the Social Development Commission, Jamaica National Building Society, and Jamaica Intellectual Property Office).[9] Hence, the Jamaican state actively inscribes Maroons into the space of the state.

Other means of entanglement are through Jamaican state financial investments in the Maroon communities. The state has invested monetarily in Maroon communities over the years and taken an active part in preserving and protecting Maroon heritage for mutual economic benefit. For instance, the Tourism Product Development Company Limited (TPDCo), working with Moore Town and Accompong Town, assisted with infrastructure, human resources, and other activities to develop the heritage tourist trade in the early 2000s.[10] In 2012, the Forest Conservation Fund planned the revitalization of a seven-mile trail from Accompong to Quick Step.[11] Around the same time, The Social Investment Fund assisted Charles Town Maroons in rehabilitating the Asafo Yard, Museum, and bathroom facilities for their project to expand heritage tourism in the community.[12]

For the Maroons, there is a reality of incorporation into the Jamaican state structure. However, there is also the symbolic significance of sovereignty claims, for all the reasons discussed above. The issue is how the conflicts that ensue are dealt with and negotiated. The state cannot fully undermine the legitimacy of the sovereignty claims (without attacking the Jamaican state's own claims about the beginning of the Jamaican nation) and the Maroons cannot escape their entanglement with the state. The Jamaican state needs the Maroons to sustain their narrative of nationhood that makes it so that the two are entangled in each other's existence. This is the dilemma.

Maroons' critical practice of sovereignty is pitted against the reality of their entanglement with the modern Jamaican state. These politics and critical practices are the manner in which they assert sovereignty through the use of African authenticity that instantiates them into the space of the African Diaspora. The state, on the other hand, sees Maroons as integral to its own claim of sovereignty, and hence Maroons are claimed to be under state jurisdiction. But forms of collaboration with the state are interpreted differently by the Maroons and the Jamaican state.

Although Maroons are entangled with and inscribed into the Jamaican state, Maroons, through the articulation of Diaspora, critically practice sovereignty. Maroons claim sovereignty and support these claims by carving out negotiated spheres of autonomy that are constantly changing. It is a politics of representation. Maroon blackness is enunciated through claims to authentic African practice. Non-Maroon African descendants in the New World authenticate their blackness through their collective histories of slavery. This history cannot be erased. In the same way, the history of the claims of sovereignty for Maroons cannot be erased. Maroons make claims to sovereignty as the basis of black humanity.

Maroons believe that possessing still-binding blood Treaties and having a unique history make it possible for them to continue to claim sovereignty, if not its full realization. They want to preserve the material conditions upon which these claims are made, such as authority over land.

Maroons struggle to have their sovereignty further recognized in the international realm. In 1984, former Colonel Harris Cawley (1984–1988) attempted to have the United Nations recognize the community as a sovereign nation but it was unsuccessful. In 2008, the then Colonel Sidney Peddie (1998–2009) worked on acknowledging the community's independence through the United Nations as well.[13]

Maroons often engage directly with international and intergovernmental bodies and organizations. Although not recognized as sovereign, Maroons often operate as independent communities and have established international relations with several external national bodies or agencies, including ones with Canada, Ghana, Japan, Nigeria, Suriname, and the United States. There are also relations with intergovernmental agencies such as the African Union, European Union, and United Nations.[14] Maroons engage in the critical practice as a sovereign group in at least symbolic relations with these entities.

The African Diaspora plays a role through the linkages in which the community is involved in creating the conditions of sovereignty. Politically, the community is engaged in international relations that allow it some autonomy from state authority. Economically, these linkages produce revenue and income-earning opportunities independent of the state and of state control.

Overall, Maroon communities are the legacies of not only resistance to slavery but collaborations among diverse peoples attempting to resist colonialism and the Western hegemonic order. At the same time, in attempting to self-govern, Maroons have been conscripted and considered collaborators in the very system of slavery and colonialism they were resisting. The path to self-determination does not follow a straight trajectory of resisting and overcoming, but one of intermittent victories and setbacks in a shifting terrain in a complicated racist geopolitical order that is difficult to escape fully. Nevertheless, these communities resulted from the desire of peoples to make a home in a difficult environment after enduring displacement, slavery, and colonialism. These communities led to the emergence of distinctively unique people on the island of Jamaica.

In claiming sovereignty, Jamaican Maroons envision a new type of state and political order. It is a desire to center freedom as a core societal value. It is a vision of and living in communal-held territory. It is the valuing of harmonious relations with environmental spaces. It is the aspiration to make the ancestors, the living, and the future generations active members of the nation. It is a globe of mobile populations that encourages diasporic and transnational networks and links. It is interdependency between states without hegemonic outcomes. It is a world that recognizes the full humanity of the African.

Maroons seek sovereignty from the large and overbearing logic of the rigid structure of the dominant and hegemonic nation-states and geo-political order, commonly critiqued as alienating. It is secession from sovereignties of post-colonial and neo-colonial states that are still under Western dominance. It is separation from an unsustainable developmentalist global order that is increasingly leading to humankind's inability to live on the planet.

The Workings of Diaspora advances that Jamaican Maroon communities, as part of African diasporic formation, operate through political mobilizations that enable people to reposition themselves and assert sovereignty in a complex global order. Examining Maroon communities as a political phenomenon that has emerged in response to the modern and increasingly globalized world illustrates the importance of diasporic formations. Maroon societies present numerous points of entry for understanding, at the micro-social level, the ways in which the least visible and most politically vulnerable communities, globally, work against the prevailing discourses of political and social formations and, instead, demonstrate the broader and global contestations of the meanings, purposes, and effectiveness of engaging alternative formations.

The idea of the African Diaspora has played a significant role in the lives of Maroons and other peoples of African descent. The critical practice of the African Diaspora of Maroon communities is one of the many means of African-descended peoples securing alternative places of sovereignty outside the confines of the currently popular model of the state. If Brazil, as one of the global economic rising BRICS nations, is any indication of future African diasporic maneuverings, the growing visibility and recognition of hundreds of quilombos (Maroon communities) in that country may be re-asserting promising alternative sites of political freedom. Perhaps this is an opening of another competing alternative space for the greater African-descended peoples in the quest for political sovereignty in an oppressive global order. In these spaces, one comprehends how African-descended communities, epitomized in this study by Maroon communities, engage "abjection," "origin," and "collective consciousness" in the modern world in order to fulfill the central goal of gaining and maintaining political freedoms.

Maroon formation as a phenomenon highlights the significance of the African Diaspora. As Neil Roberts rightly contends, marronage is crucial to understanding the black New World and diasporic societies.[15] The act or performance of marronage is one of many means of living the African Diaspora as critical practice, articulation, and politics. Politically, marronage and Diaspora are spaces of freedom that challenge a variety of hegemonic authorities, including those found in slavery, colonialism, nation-states, neo-colonialism, and economic globalization.

Notes

1. Melville Currie, interview by author, Accompong Town, St. Elizabeth, Jamaica, August 14, 2012.
2. "Maroons Have No Special Rights under Jamaican Laws," *Jamaica Gleaner* (Kingston), February 10, 1973.
3. Horace Hines, "Maroons Demand Autonomy 'We Want to be Recognised by Jamaican Constitution,' Says Maroon Chief," *Jamaica Observer* (Kingston), January 13, 2011, accessed December 4, 2012, http://www.jamaicaobserver.com/pfversion/Maroons-demand-autonomy_8288186.
4. Albert Ferguson, "Ratify our Sovereignty, Maroon Leader Urges State," *Jamaica Gleaner* (Kingston), January 09, 2020, accessed March 24, 2020, http://jamaica-gleaner.com/article/news/20200109/ratify-our-sovereignty-Maroon-leader-urges-state.
5. "Accompong Maroons Urged to Preserve History," *JIS News* (Kingston), January 13, 2009, accessed December 4, 2012, http://jis.gov.jm/accompong-Maroons-urged-to-preserve-history/.
6. "Thousands Celebrate With the Maroons," *JIS News* (Kingston), January 9, 2012, accessed March 12, 2013, http://jis.gov.jm/thousands-celebrate-with-the-Maroons/;

Horace Hines, "Maroon Celebrations Kick Starts 'Jamaica 50,'" *Jamaica Observer* (Kingston), January 19, 2012, accessed March 12, 2013, http://www.jamaicaobserver.com/pfversion/Maroon-celebrations-kick-starts--Jamaica-50-_10588223.

7. "Minister Hanna Calls for Return to Traditional Values," *JIS News* (Kingston), January 7, 2013, accessed March 12, 2013, http://jis.gov.jm/minister-hanna-calls-for-return-to-traditional-values/.

8. "Minister Hanna to Engage Maroon Communities in Cultural Mission," *JIS News* (Kingston), January 9, 2013, accessed March 12, 2013, http://jis.gov.jm/minister-hanna-to-engage-Maroon-communities-in-cultural-mission/.

9. Garfield Rowe, interview by author, Accompong Town, St. Elizabeth, Jamaica, January 10, 2013; Garfield Myers, "Maroons Prepared to Die for Cockpit, Says Colonel Peddie," *Jamaica Observer* (Kingston), January 4, 2007, accessed December 4, 2012, http://www.jamaicaobserver.com/pfversion/117440_Maroons-prepared-to-die-for-Cockpit--says-Colonel-Peddie; Currie, interview; "Maroons Gear up for Annual Celebrations," *JIS News* (Kingston), January 3, 2005, accessed December 4, 2012, http://jis.gov.jm/Maroons-gear-up-for-annual-celebrations/; "Accompong Town gets Internet Café," *Jamaica Observer* (Kingston), March 24, 2011, accessed December 4, 2012, http://www.jamaicaobserver.com/pfversion/Accompong-Town-gets-Internet-cafe_8532767; "Junitavan Lagoon in Accompong to be Restored," *JIS News* (Kingston), August 13, 2008, accessed December 4, 2012, http://jis.gov.jm/junitavan-lagoon-in-accompong-to-be-restored/; "JIPO Paves Way for Growth by Protecting Intellectual Property Rights," *JIS News* (Kingston), May 4, 2009, accessed December 4, 2012, http://jis.gov.jm/jipo-paves-way-for-growth-by-protecting-intellectual-property-rights/; "Govt. to Focus on Cultural Industries," *JIS News* (Kingston), March 28, 2008, accessed December 4, 2012, http://jis.gov.jm/govt-to-focus-on-cultural-industries/; Peter Kavanaugh, "Maroons Fight to Preserve Tradition," *Jamaica Gleaner* (Kingston), May 3, 2008.

10. "Moore Town Maroon Village to Be Part of Tourism Product," *Jamaica Observer* (Kingston), February 15, 2002, accessed December 4, 2012, http://www.jamaicaobserver.com/pfversion/21309_Moore-Town-Maroon-Village-to-be-part-of-tourism-product; Petre Williams, "Leveraging History," *Jamaica Observer* (Kingston), August 18, 2002, accessed December 4, 2012, http://www.jamaicaobserver.com/pfversion/30566_Leveraging-History.

11. "Fresh Lease on Life for Maroon Trail," *Jamaica Gleaner* (Kingston), June 30, 2012.

12. "Charles Town Maroons Get $18m For Asafo Yard Rehab," *Jamaica Gleaner* (Kingston), June 27, 2012.

13. "Maroon Indigenous People Seeking Autonomy in Jamaica," *Caribbean Media Corporation News Agency* (Bridgetown, Barbados), January 8, 2008.

14. Ferron Williams, interview by author, Accompong Town, St. Elizabeth, Jamaica, January 7, 2012; Garfield Rowe, interview; Harris Cawley, interview by author, Accompong Town, St. Elizabeth, Jamaica, August 1, 2012; Wallace Sterling, interview by author, Moore Town, Portland, Jamaica, December 1, 2011.

15. Neil Roberts, *Freedom as Marronage* (Chicago: The University of Chicago Press, 2015), 3–4.

Appendix 1

Leeward Maroon and British Treaty

THE FOLLOWING IS THE TREATY SIGNED between the British colonists and the Leeward Maroons.

At the camp near Trelawny Town
March the 1st, 1738–9.

In the name of God, Amen. Whereas captain Cudjoe, captain Accompong, captain Johnny, captain Cuffee, captain Quaco, and several other negroes, their dependents and adherents, have been in a state of war and hostility for several years past against our sovereign lord the king, and the inhabitants of this island; and whereas peace and friendship amongst mankind, and the preventing of effusion of blood, is agreeable to God, constant to reason, and desired by every good man; and whereas his majesty George the second, King of Great Britain, France, and Ireland, and of Jamaica lord, defender of faith, etc. has by letters patent, dated February the twenty-fourth, one thousand seven hundred and thirty eight, in the twelfth year of his reign, granted full power and authority to John Guthrie and Francis Sadler, esquires, to negotiate and finally conclude a treaty of peace and friendship with the aforesaid Cudjoe, the rest of his captains, adherents, and others his men; they, mutually, sincerely, and amicably have agreed to the following articles:

First, That all hostilities shall cease on both sides for ever.

Secondly, That the said captain Cudjoe, the rest of his captains, adherents and men, shall be for ever hereafter in a perfect state of freedom and liberty, expecting those who have been taken by them, or fled to them within the two years last past, if such are willing to return to their said masters and owners, with full pardon and indemnity, from their said masters and owners for what is past; provided always, that if they are not willing to return, they shall remain in subjection to captain Cudjoe, and his friendship with us, according to the form and tenor of this treaty.

Thirdly, That they shall enjoy and possess for themselves and posterity for ever, all the lands situate and lying between Trelawny Town and the Cockpits, to the amount of fifteen hundred acres, bearing north-west from the said Trelawny Town.

Fourthly, That they shall have liberty to plant the said lands with coffee, cocoa, ginger, tobacco, and cotton, and to breed cattle, hogs, goats, or any other stock, and dispose of the produce or increase of the said commodities to the inhabitants of this island; provided always, that they bring the said commodities to market, they shall apply first to the customs, or any other magistrate of the respective parishes where they expose their goods for sale, for license to vend the same.

Fifthly, That captain Cudjoe, and all the captain's adherents, and people not in subjection to him, shall all live together within the bounds of Trelawny Town; and that they have liberty to hunt where they shall think fit, except within three miles of any settlement, crawl or pen; provided always, that in case of hunters of captain Cudjoe, and those of other settlements meet, then the hogs to be equally divided between both parties.

Sixthly, That the said captain Cudjoe, and his successors, do use their best endeavors to take, kill, suppress or destroy, either by themselves or jointly, with any other number of men commanded on that service by his excellency the governor or commander in chief for the time being, all rebels wheresoever they be throughout this island, unless they submit to the same terms of accommodation granted to captain Cudjoe, and his successors.

Seventhly, That in case this island be invaded by any foreign enemy, the said captain Cudjoe, and his successors herein after named, or to be appointed, shall then, upon notice given, immediately repair to any place the governor for the time being shall appoint, in order to repel the said invaders with his or their utmost force; and to submit to the orders of the commander in chief on that occasion.

Eighthly, That if any white man shall do any manner of injury to captain Cudjoe, his successors, or any of his or their people, they shall apply to any commanding officer or magistrate in the neighborhood for justice; and in case of captain Cudjoe, or any of his people, shall do any injury to any white person, he shall submit himself or deliver up such offenders to justice.

Ninthly, That if any negroes shall hereafter run away from their masters or owners, and fall into captain Cudjoe's hands, they shall immediately sent back to the chief magistrate of the next parish where they are taken; and those that bring them are to be satisfied for their trouble, as the legislature shall appoint.

Tenthly, That all negroes taken since the raising of this party by captain Cudjoe's people, shall immediately be returned.

Eleventhly, That captain Cudjoe, and his successors, shall wait on his Excellency, or commander in chief for the time being, every year, if thereunto required.

Twelfth, That captain Cudjoe, during his life, and the captains succeeding him, shall have full power to inflict any punishments they think proper for crimes committed by their men among themselves, death only excepted; in which case, if the captain thinks they deserve death, he shall be obliged to bring them before any justice of the peace, who shall order proceedings on their trial equal to those of other free negroes.

Thirteenth, That Captain Cudjoe with his people shall cut, clear and keep open, large, and convenient roads from Trelawny Town to Westmoreland and St. James's, and if possible to St. Elizabeth's.

Fourteenth, That two white men to be nominated by his excellency, or the commander in chief for the time being, shall constantly live and reside with captain Cudjoe and his successors, in order to maintain a friendly correspondence with the inhabitants of this island.

Fifteenth, That captain Cudjoe shall, during his life, be chief commander in Trelawny Town, after his decease the command to devolve on his brother captain Accompong; and in case of his decease, on his next brother captain Johnny; and, failing him, captain Cuffee shall succeed, who is to be succeeded by captain Quaco, and after all their demises, the governor or commander in chief for that time being, shall appoint from time to time whom he thinks fit for that command.

In testimony of the above presents, we have hereunto set out hands and seal the day and date above written.

John Guthrie (L.S.)
Francis Sadler (L.S.)

The mark X of Captain Cudjoe

Appendix 2

Windward Maroon and British Treaty

THE FOLLOWING IS THE TEXT of the second written treaty with the Windward Maroons.

Whereas his Excellency Edward Trelawny, esquire; governor and chief in command of the island aforesaid, hath given power and authority to colonel Robert Bennett to treat with the rebellious negroes, this day, being the twenty-third day of June, one thousand seven hundred and thirty-nine, captain Quao, and several other under his command, surrendered under the following terms, viz.

First, That all hostilities on both sides shall cease for ever, Amen.

Secondly, That captain Quao and his people shall have a certain quantity of land given to them, in order to raise provisions, hogs, fowls, goats, or whatsoever stock they may think proper, sugar-canes except, saving for their hogs, and to have liberty to sell the same.

Thirdly, That four white men shall constantly live and reside with them in their town, in order to keep a good correspondence with the inhabitants of this island.

Fourthly, That captain Quao and his people shall be ready on all commands the governor or the commander in chief for the time being shall send him, to suppress and destroy all other party and parties of rebellious negroes, that now are or shall from time to time gather together or settle in any part of the island, and shall bring in such other negroes as shall from time to time run away from their respective owners, from the date of these articles.

Fifthly, That the said captain Quao and his people shall also be ready to assist his excellency the governor for the time being, in case of any invasion, and shall put himself, with all his people that are able to bear arms, under the command of the general or commander of such forces, appointed by his excellency to defend the island from the said invasion.

Sixthly, That the said captain Quao and his people shall be in subjection to his excellency the governor for the time being, and the said captain Quao shall once every year, or oftener, appear before the governor, if thereunto required.

Seventhly, That in case any of the hunters belonging to the inhabitants of this island, and the hunters belonging to captain Quao, should meet, in order to hinder all disputes, captain Quao will order his people to let the inhabitant's hunters have the hog.

Eighthly, That in case captain Quao and his people shall take up any runaway negroes that shall abscond from their respective owners, he or they shall carry them to their respective masters or owners, and shall be paid for so doing, as the legislature shall appoint.

Ninthly, That in case captain Quao and his people should be disturbed by a greater number of rebels than he is able to fight, that then he shall be assisted by as many white people as the governor for the time being shall think proper.

Tenthly, That in case any of the negroes belonging to captain Quao shall be guilty of any crime or crimes that may deserve death, he shall deliver him up to the next magistrate, in order to be tried as other negroes are; but small crimes he may punish himself.

Eleventhly, That in case any white man, or other inhabitants of this islands, shall disturb or annoy any of the people, hogs, stock or whatsoever goods may belong to the said captain Quao, or any of his people, when they come down to the settlements to vend the same, upon due complaint made to a magistrate he or they shall have justice done them.

Twelfth, That neither captain Quao, nor any of his people shall bring any hogs, fowls, or any other kind of stock or provisions to sell to the inhabitants, without a ticket from under the hand of one or more of the white men residing within their town.

Thirteenth, That captain Quao nor any of his people, shall hunt within three miles of any settlement.

Fourteenth, That in case captain Quao should die, that then the command of his people shall descend to captain Thomboy, and at his death to descend to captain Apong, and at his death to captain Blackwell shall succeed, and at his death captain Clash shall succeed; and when he dies, the governor or commander in chief for the time being shall appoint whom he thinks proper.

In Witness to these articles, the above-named colonel Robert Bennett and captain Quao have set their hands and seals the day and year above written.

Robert Bennett. (L.S.)
The mark of X Captain Quao

Appendix 3

Table A3.1. Partial List of Colonels/Chiefs of Jamaican Maroon Communities

Colonel/Chief	*Tenure*
	Accompong Town
Cudjoe, Sr.?	–
Cudjoe (Kojo)	c. 1720–c.1764
Accompong (Akyeampong)	c. 1739–c.1770s
Crankey?	c. 1770s
Austin	c. 1797–c. 1808
White	–
Foster?	c. 1820s
T. Crosse	–
Wright?	–
H. D. Rowe	c. 1870–c.1880
R. J. McLeod?	–
K. T. Wright	c. 1904
H. E. Wright	c. 1904–1920
H. R. Rowe	1920–c.1930s
Thomas. J. Cawley?	c. 1930s
Edgar Rowe?	c. 1940s
James Rowe?	c. 1940s
Walter James Robertson	c.1943–c. 1949
Isaac Myles	c. 1950s
Thomas. J. Cawley	c. 1949–1957
Walter James Robertson	1957–1967
Martin-Luther Wright	1967–1984
Charles Reid?	–

(continued)

Table A3.1. *(continued)*

Colonel/Chief	*Tenure*
Harris N. Cawley	1984–1988
Martin-Luther Wright	1988–1993
Meredith Rowe	1993–1998
Sidney Peddie	1998–2009
Ferron Williams	2009–
Charles Town	
Quao	–
Cain	–
George Gray	–
Afee Cudjoe	c. 1796
Samuel (James) Grant	c. 1796–c. 1808
George Oliver Gordon	c. 1820
Nathaniel Beckford	c. 1830–c.1840
Rashford	c. 1898–1901
Samuel Charles	c. 1938
Jestina 'Tun-Tun' Campbell?	–
–	–
Frank Lumsden	2004–2015
Marcia Douglas	c. 2015–
Crawford Town	
Quao	c. 1740–c. 1746
Edward (Ned) Crawford	c. 1746–c.1754
Cudjoe Town/Trelawny Town	
Cudjoe (Sr.)?	–
Cudjoe (Kojo)	c. 1739–c. 1763/4
Lewis	c. 1763/4
Cuffee	–
Tuluppanny	–
Robin	–
Long Quashee	–
Cudjoe	c. 1767
Montague James	c. 1792–1811/2
Moore Town/New Nanny Town	
Welcome	c. 1738–c. 1760
Grandy Nanny	c. 1740–c. 1742
Clash	c. 1760–c. 1767
Sambo	c. 1760–c. 1770s
Charles Harris	c. 1797
John Sambo	c. 1807
John Ellis	c. 1808
Kean Osbourne	c. 1830
Robert Osborne	c. 1865
George McKenzie	c. 1840
Wallen Ellis?	c. 1898
–	–

Colonel/Chief	Tenure
James Harrison	–
Leslie Harrison	c. 1940s
James Searchwell	c. 1940s–c.1946
E. A. Downer	c. 1946–c. 1964
C. L. R. Harris	1964–1995
Wallace Sterling	1995–
Scot's Hall	
Cudjoe	c. 1760–c. 1793
George Gray	c. 1791
John Gordon	c. 1807–c. 1809
Peter Ellis	c. 1809
John Crawford	c. 1820
Robert Nugent	c. 1840
Philip Lattibeaudiere	c. 1959–c.1983
Noel Prehay	c. 1983–2016
Rudolph Pink	2016–

Sources: Currie, interview; Reid, interview; Lumsden, interview; Sterling, interview; Williams, interview; Carey, *Maroon Story*, 448, 527, 551, and 552; Sivapragasam, "After the Treaties," 61, 74, 172, 271, 272, and 273; Kopytoff, "The Maroons of Jamaica," 172, 202, 203, 286–87, 325, 326, 329, 330, 332, and 333; Bilby, *True-Born Maroon*, 191; Accompong Town Maroon Community, "Sovereign State of Accompong Maroons," accessed May 27, 2020, https://www.accompong-gov.org/maroon-council-ministries; Wright, "Accompong Maroons of Jamaica," 70; "Maroons Celebrate: Bicentenary of Freedom," *Daily Gleaner* (Kingston), March 5, 1938, 17; "Split which has taken place between Maroons," *Daily Gleaner* (Kingston), September 1, 1938, 9; "Colonel of Maroons," *Daily Gleaner* (Kingston), December 2, 1921, 2; "Surveyor Gone Down To Accompong Lands," *Daily Gleaner* (Kingston), September 8, 1938, 4; Ted Glave, "Colonel and New Leader of The Maroons Named," *Daily Gleaner* (Kingston), February 7, 1949, 11; "Accompong Maroons at odds over election of colonel," *Daily Gleaner* (Kingston), July 19, 1967, 26; "Maroons pick new Colonel," *Daily Gleaner* (Kingston), November 17, 1967, 1; "Detective is new Maroon Colonel," *Jamaica Gleaner* (Kingston), September 25, 1993, 3; "Sidney Peddie new Maroon Chief of Accompong," *Jamaica Gleaner* (Kingston), December 12, 1998, A3; W. Rashford, "Maroons Deplore the Queen's Death," *Daily Gleaner* (Kingston), February 1, 1901, 7; "Acting Governor's Tour," *Daily Gleaner* (Kingston), October 27, 1898, 1; Paul H. Williams, "Colonel Lumsden – Maroon vanguard," *Jamaica Gleaner* (Kingston), July 2, 2007, A6; Orantes Moore, "Scott's Hall maroons get new colonel," *Jamaica Jamaica Gleaner* (Kingston), June 1, 2016, accessed December 21, 2020, https://jamaica-gleaner.com/article/news/20160602/scotts-hall-maroons-get-new-colonel; "Accompong Maroons at Odds of Colonel," *Jamaica Gleaner* (Kingston), July 19, 1967, 1; "Maroons Mark Treaty with UK in Festive Mood," *Daily Gleaner* (Kingston), January 7, 1985, 1; "All Set for Maroon Election," *Jamaica Gleaner* (Kingston), May 22, 2004, A7.

Bibliography

Accompong News (@AccompongNews). Twitter, December 30, 2020. https://twitter.com/AccompongNews.

Accompong Town Maroon Community. "Sovereign State of Accompong Maroons." Accessed May 29, 2020. https://www.accompong-gov.org/.

Accompong Traditional Medicinal Creative Group and Youth Project. *Maroon Traditional Medicine*. Accompong Town, St. Elizabeth, Jamaica, [publisher not identified] 1994.

Afroz, Sultana. "From Moors to Marronage: The Islamic Heritage of the Maroons in Jamaica." *Journal of Muslim Minority Affairs* 19, no. 2 (1999): 161–179.

——. "The Manifestation of Tawhid: The Muslim Heritage of the Maroons in Jamaica." *Caribbean Quarterly* 45, no. 1 (1999): 27–40.

Agorsah, E. Kofi, ed. *Maroon Heritage Archaeological, Ethnographic, and Historical Perspectives*. Barbados: Canoe Press, 1994.

Akyeampong, Emmanuel Kwaku. "Africans in the Diaspora: The Diaspora and Africa." *African Affairs: The Journal of the Royal African Society* 99, no. 395 (2000): 183–215.

Alleyne, Mervyn C. and Beverley Hall-Alleyne. "Language Maintenance and Language Death in the Caribbean." *Caribbean Quarterly* 28, no. 4 (1982): 52–59.

Anderson, Roy T. *Akwantu: The Journey*. [United States]: Action 4 Reel Filmworks, 2012. DVD.

——. *Queen Nanny: Legendary Maroon Chieftainess*. [United States]: Action 4 Reel Filmworks and Kanopy, 2016. DVD.

Arrom, José Juan and Manuel Antonio García Arévalo. *Cimarron*. Santo Domingo, Dominican Republic: [s.n.] 1986.

Ashcraft, Richard. "Hobbes's Natural Man: A Study in Ideology Formation." *The Journal of Politics* 33, no. 4 (Nov. 1971): 1076–1117.

Ashcroft, Michael. "Robert Charles Dallas: Identified as the Author of an Anonymous Book About Jamaica." *Jamaica Journal* no. 44 (1979): 96–98.

Bastide, Roger. *African Civilisations in the New World.* New York: Harper & Row, 1971.

Bauböck, Rainer, and Thomas Faist. *Diaspora and Transnationalism: Concepts, Theories and Methods.* Amsterdam: Amsterdam University Press, 2010.

Beckles, Hilary. "From Land to Sea: Runway Barbados Slaves and Servants, 1630–1700." In *Out of the House of Bondage: Runaways, Resistance and Maroonage in Africa and the New World*, edited by Gad J. Heuman, 79–94. London: Cass, 1986.

Bilby, Kenneth M. *Drums of Defiance: Maroon Music from the Earliest Free Black Communities of Jamaica.* Washington, DC: Smithsonian Folkways, 1992.

———. "How the Older Heads Talk: A Jamaican Maroon Spirit Possession Language and Its Relationship to the Creoles of Suriname and Sierra Leone." *New West Indian Guide* 57 (1983): 37–88.

———. "The Kromanti Dance of the Windward Maroons of Jamaica." *New West Indian Guide* 55, no. 1 (1981): 52–101.

———. "Making Modernity in the Hinterlands: New Maroon Musics in the Black Atlantic." *Popular Music* 19, no. 3 (2000): 265–292.

———. "Maroon Autonomy in Jamaica." *Cultural Survival Quarterly* 25, no. 4 (2002): 26–31.

———. "Swearing by the Past, Swearing to the Future: Sacred Oaths, Alliances, and Treaties Among the Guianese and Jamaican Maroons." *Ethnohistory* 44, no. 4 (1997): 655–690.

———. *True-Born Maroons.* Gainesville: University Press of Florida, 2005.

———. "Two Sister Pikni: A Historical Tradition of Dual Ethnogenesis in Eastern Jamaica." *Caribbean Quarterly* 30 (1984): 10–25.

Bodin, Jean. *On Sovereignty: Four Chapters from the Six Books of the Commonwealth.* Edited by Julian H. Franklin. Cambridge [England]: Cambridge University Press, 1992.

Brown, J. N. "Black Europe and the African Diaspora: A Discourse on Location." In *Black Europe and the African Diaspora*, edited by Darlene Clark Hine, Trica Danielle Keaton, and Stephen Small, 201–211. Urbana: University of Illinois Press, 2009.

Brymner, Douglas. *The Jamaica Maroons How They Came to Nova Scotia: How They Left It.* [place of publication not identified]: [publisher not identified], 1894.

Butler, Kim D. "Defining Diaspora, Refining a Discourse." *Diaspora: A Journal of Transnational Studies* 10, no. 2 (2001): 189–219.

Campbell, Mavis Christine. *The Maroons of Jamaica, 1655–1796: A History of Resistance, Collaboration & Betrayal.* Granby, MA: Bergin & Garvey, 1988.

———. "Marronage in Jamaica: Its Origin in the Seventeenth Century." *Annals of the New York Academy of Sciences* 292, no. 1 (1977): 389–419.

———. *Nova Scotia and the Fighting Maroons: A Documentary History.* [Williamsburg, VA]: [Department of Anthropology, College of William and Mary], 1990.

Campbell, Mavis Christine and George Ross. *Back to Africa: George Ross and the Maroons: from Nova Scotia to Sierra Leone.* Trenton, NJ: Africa World Press, 1993.

Carey, Bev. *The Maroon Story: The Authentic and Original History of the Maroons in the History of Jamaica, 1490–1880*. Gordon Town, Jamaica: Agouti Press, 1997.

CaribNation TV. "The Jamaican Maroons." Accessed November 23, 2020. https://www.youtube.com/watch?v=-US3_OxhEsk.

Cawley, Harris. Interview by author. Accompong Town, St. Elizabeth, Jamaica. August 1, 2012.

———. *The Sound of the Abeng: A Short Synopsis on the Accompong Maroons*. Accompong Town, Jamaica: Speedy Prints, 1986.

Chambers, James. Interview by the author. Accompong Town, St. Elizabeth, Jamaica. December 22, 2011.

Charles Town Maroon Community. @ctmaroons. Twitter, December 30, 2020. https://twitter.com/ctmaroons.

Charles Town Maroon Community. "Charles Town Maroon Community." Accessed May 29, 2020. http://www.maroons-jamaica.com/q/index.php/home.

Clifford, James. "Diasporas." *Cultural Anthropology* 9, no. 3 (1994): 302–38.

Cohen, Milton. "Medical Beliefs and Practices of the Maroons of Moore Town: A Study in Acculturation." PhD diss., New York University, 1978.

Comaroff, Jean and John Comaroff. *Of Revelation and Revolution: Christianity, Colonialism, and Consciousness in South Africa, Vol. 1*. Chicago: University of Chicago Press, 1991.

Connell, Robert J. "Maroon Ecology: Land, Sovereignty, and Environmental Justice." *The Journal of Latin American and Caribbean Anthropology* 25, no. 2 (June 2019): 218–235.

Craton, Michael. *Testing the Chains: Resistance to Slavery in the British West Indies*. Ithaca, [N.Y.]: Cornell University Press, 1982.

Currie, Melville. Interview by author. Accompong Town, St. Elizabeth, Jamaica. December 23, 2011.

Curtain, Marguerite. *Nanny, Queen of the Maroons*. [Kingston, Jamaica]: Ministry of Education, 1975.

Dalby, David. "Ashanti Survivals in the Language and Traditions of the Windward Maroons of Jamaica." *African Language Studies* no. 12 (1971): 31–51.

Dallas, Robert Charles. *The History of the Maroons, from Their Origin to the Establishment of Their Chief Tribe at Sierra Leone*. London: T. N. Longman and O. Rees, 1803.

DjeDje, Jacqueline C. "Remembering Kojo: History, Music, and Gender in the January Sixth Celebration of the Jamaican Accompong Maroons." *Black Music Research Journal* 18, no. 1/2 (1998): 67–120.

Douglas, Marcia. Interview by the author, Charles Town, Portland, Jamaica. December 1, 2011.

Douglass, Frederick. *Narrative of the Life of Frederick Douglass, an American Slave; My Bondage and My Freedom; Life and Times of Frederick Douglass*. New York: Literary Classics of the United States, 1994.

Du Bois, William E. B. and Brent Hayes Edwards. *The Souls of Black Folk*. Oxford: Oxford University Press, 2007.

Dunham, Katherine and Ted Cook. *Katherine Dunham's Journey to Accompong.* New York: Henry Holt, 1946.

Edwards, Brent Hayes. *The Practice of Diaspora: Literature, Translation, and the Rise of Black Internationalism.* Cambridge, MA: Harvard University Press, 2003.

———. "The Uses of Diaspora." *Social Text* 19, no. 1 (2001): 3–38.

Edwards, Bryan. *The History, Civil and Commercial, of the British Colonies in the West Indies: in two volumes.* London: Printed for John Stockdale, 1794.

"Edwards, Bryan." *The History of Parliament Online.* Accessed March 27, 2020. http://www.historyofparliamentonline.org/volume/1790-1820/member/edwards-bryan-1743-1800.

Edwards, Bryan. *The Proceedings of the Governor and Assembly of Jamaica, in regard to the Maroon negroes: to which is prefixed, an introductory account, containing observations on the disposition, character, manners, and habits of life of the Maroons, and a detail of the origin, progress, and termination of the late war between those people and the white inhabitants.* London: Printed for J. Stockdale, 1796.

Edwards, Bryan, and William Young. *An Historical Survey of the Island of Saint Domingo Together with an Account of the Maroon Negroes in the Island of Jamaica, and a History of the War in the West Indies, in 1793, and 1794.* London: Printed for John Stockdale, 1801.

Eltis, David. *The Rise of African Slavery in the Americas.* Cambridge, UK: Cambridge University Press, 2000.

Festival of American Folklife. *1992 Festival of American Folklife: June 25–June 29; July 2– July 5.* [Washington, DC]: The Institution, 1992.

Fiske, John. "Open the Hallway: Some Remarks on the Fertility of Stuart Hall's Contribution to Critical Theory." In *Stuart Hall: Critical Dialogues in Cultural Studies,* edited by David Morley and Kuan-Hsing Chen, 212-220. New York: Taylor & Francis, 1996, 212–220.

Fortin, J. A. "'Blackened Beyond Our Native Hue': Removal, Identity and the Trelawney Maroons on the Margins of the Atlantic World, 1796–1801." *Citizenship Studies* 10, no. 1 (2006): 5–34.

Foster, Ikamellia. Interview by author. Accompong Town, St. Elizabeth, Jamaica. December 30, 2011.

Galloway, Ernestine. "Religious Beliefs and Practices of Maroon Children of Jamaica." Ph.D. diss., New York University, 1985.

Gilroy, Paul. *The Black Atlantic: Modernity and Double Consciousness.* Cambridge, MA: Harvard University Press, 1993.

Gomez, Michael Angelo. *Exchanging Our Country Marks: The Transformation of African Identities in the Colonial and Antebellum South.* Chapel Hill: University of North Carolina Press, 1998.

Gottlieb, Karla Lewis. *The Mother of Us All: A History of Queen Nanny, Leader of the Windward Jamaican Maroons.* Trenton, NJ: Africa World Press, 2000.

Grossberg, Lawrence. "On Postmodernism and Articulation: An Interview with Stuart Hall." In *Stuart Hall: Critical Dialogues in Cultural Studies,* edited by David Morley and Kuan-Hsing Chen, 131–150. New York: Taylor & Francis, 1996.

Hall, Gwendolyn Midlo. *Slavery and African Ethnicities in the Americas Restoring the Links*. Chapel Hill: The University of North Carolina Press. 2009.

Hall, Neville A. T. and B. W. Higman. *Slave Society in the Danish West Indies: St. Thomas, St. John, and St. Croix*. Baltimore: Johns Hopkins University Press, 1992.

Hall, Stuart. "Cultural Identity and Diaspora." In *Identity: Community, Culture, Difference*, edited by Jonathan Rutherford, 222–237. London: Lawrence & Wishart, 1990.

———. "New Cultures for Old." *In A Place in the World?: Places, Cultures and Globalization*, edited by John Allen and Doreen B. Massey, 175–214. Oxford: Oxford University Press, 1995.

———. "Old and New Identities, Old and New Ethnicities." In *Theories of Race and Racism: A Reader*, edited by John Solomos and Les Back, 144–153. London: Routledge, 2001.

———. "The Problem of Ideology: Marxism without Guarantees." In *Stuart Hall: Critical Dialogues in Cultural Studies*, edited by David Morley and Kuan-Hsing Chen, 25–46. New York: Taylor & Francis, 1996.

———. 1999. "Thinking the Diaspora: Home-Thoughts from Abroad." *Small Axe: A Journal of Criticism* no. 6: 1–18.

Hall-Alleyne, Beverley. "Asante Kotoko: The Maroons of Jamaica." *Newsletter: African-Caribbean Institute of Jamaica* (1982): 3–40.

Harris, C. L. G. *The Chieftainess: Glimpses of Grandy Nanny (Rt. Excellent Nanny of the Maroons)*. Huntsville, Alabama: Publishing Designs, 2009.

———. "The Maroons and Moore Town." *In Festival of American Folklife: June 25–June 29; July 2–July 5*. Washington, DC: Smithsonian Institution, 1992.

———. *Teacha*. Huntsville, Alabama: Publishing Designs, 2004.

———. "The True Traditions of my Ancestors." In *Maroon Heritage: Archaeological, Ethnographic, and Historical Perspectives*, edited by E. Kofi Agorsah, 36–63. Barbados: Canoe Press, 1994.

Harris, C. L. G. and Charles Aarons. *On My Honour: A Tale of the Maroons*. [Place of publication not identified]: [publisher not identified], 1988.

Harris, Joseph E. "Expanding the Scope of African Diaspora Studies: The Middle East and India, a Research Agenda." *Radical History Review* 87, no. 1 (2003): 157–68.

———, ed. *Global Dimensions of the African Diaspora*. Washington, DC: Howard University Press, 1982.

Herskovits, Melville J. *The Myth of the Negro Past*. Boston, MA: Beacon Press, 1958.

Heuman, Gad J. *The Killing Time: The Morant Bay Rebellion in Jamaica*. Knoxville: University of Tennessee Press, 1994.

Hintzen, Percy C. and Jean Muteba Rahier. "Introduction." In *Global Circuits of Blackness: Interrogating the African Diaspora*, edited by Jean Muteba Rahier, Percy C. Hintzen, and Felipe Smith, ix–xxvi. Urbana: University of Illinois Press, 2010.

Hobbes, Thomas. *Leviathan: With Selected Variants from the Latin Edition of 1668*. Edited by E. M. Curley. Indianapolis: Hackett Pub. Co, 1994.

Hoekstra, Kinch. "History of Political Thought." Lecture, Department of Political Science, University of California, Berkeley, April 2, 2009.

Hutchinson, Ann-Marie. Interview by author. Accompong Town, St. Elizabeth, Jamaica. December 28, 2011.

Hu-DeHart, Evelyn. "The Future of 'Diaspora' in Diaspora Studies: Has the Word Run Its Course?" *Verge: Studies in Global Asias* 1, no. 1 (2015): 38–44.

Jackson, Rachel. "The Trans-Atlantic Journey of Gumbé: Where and Why Has It Survived?" *African Music* 9, no. 2 (2012): 128–153.

Jamaica. Colonial Secretary's Office, Jamaica Archives and Record Department, Spanish Town. "T.H. to Colonial Office," October 20, 1882, Box 1/5/76/3/23.

Jean, Besson. "Folk Law and Legal Pluralism in Jamaica." *The Journal of Legal Pluralism and Unofficial Law* 31, no. 43 (1999): 31–56.

Journals of the Assembly of Jamaica, Vol. III (1731–1745). Jamaica Archives and Record Department, Spanish Town, Jamaica.

Khan, Aisha. "Material and Immaterial Bodies: Diaspora Studies and the Problem of Culture, Identity, and Race." *Small Axe* 19, no. 3 (2015): 29–49.

Kim, Sandra So Hee Chi. "Redefining Diaspora Through a Phenomenology of Postmemory." *Diaspora: A Journal of Transnational Studies* 16, no. 3 (2007): 337–352.

Konadu, Kwasi. *The Akan Diaspora in the Americas.* New York: Oxford University Press, 2010.

Kopytoff, Barbara K. "The Development of Jamaican Maroon Ethnicity." *Caribbean Quarterly* 22, no. 2–3 (1976): 33–50.

———. "The Early Political Development of Jamaican Maroon Societies." *The William and Mary Quarterly* 35, no. 2 (1978): 287–307.

———. "The Maroons of Jamaica: An Ethnohistorical Study of Incomplete Polities, 1655–1905." PhD diss., University of Pennsylvania, 1973.

———. "Religious Change Among the Jamaican Maroons: The Ascendance of the Christian God Within a Traditional Cosmology." *Journal of Social History* 20, no. 3 (1987): 463–484.

Kraynak, Robert P. "Hobbes on Barbarism and Civilization." *The Journal of Politics* 45, no. 1 (1983): 86–109.

Kristeva, Julia. *Powers of Horror: An Essay of Abjection.* New York: Columbia University Press, 1984.

La Rosa Corzo, Gabino. *Runaway Slave Settlements in Cuba: Resistance and Repression*. Chapel Hill: University of North Carolina Press, 2003.

Larrain, Jorge. "Stuart Hall and the Marxist Concept of Ideology." In *Stuart Hall: Critical Dialogues in Cultural Studies*, edited by David Morley and Kuan-Hsing Chen, 47–70. New York: Taylor & Francis, 1996.

Leigh, Devin. "The Origin of a Source: Edward Long, Coromantee Slave Revolts and The History of Jamaica." *Slavery & Abolition* 40, no. 2 (2019): 295–320.

Lewis, Earl. "To Turn as on a Pivot: Writing African Americans into a History of Overlapping Diasporas." *The American Historical Review* 100, no. 3 (1995): 765.

Locke, John. *Political Writings*. Edited by David Wootton. New York, NY: Mentor, 1993.

Lockett, J. D. "The Deportation of the Maroons of Trelawny Town to Nova Scotia, Then Back to Africa." *Journal of Black Studies* 30, no. 1 (1999): 5–14.

Long, Edward. "An Abstract of the Jamaica Code Noir, or Laws affecting Negroe and other Slaves in that Island.—And, first of, PENAL ARTICLES." 1746. File 12416. Edward Long Papers [Microfilm]. Butler Library, Columbia University, New York, NY.

——. *The History of Jamaica, or, General Survey of the Antient and Modern State of the Island: With Reflections on Its Situation Settlements, Inhabitants, Climate, Products, Commerce, Laws, and Government: Illustrated with Copper Plates*. London: T. Lowndes, 1774.

——. "The History of Jamaica to 1742." 1746. File 12416. Edward Long Papers [Microfilm]. Butler Library, Columbia University, New York, NY.

Lumsden, Frank. Interview by author. Charles Town, Portland, Jamaica. December 06, 2011.

MacClintock, Ann. *Imperial Leather: Race, Gender and Sexuality in Colonial Context*. New York: Routledge, 1995.

Machiavelli, Niccolò. *Selected Political Writings*. Translated by David Wootton. Indianapolis: Hackett Pub. Co, 1994.

Martin, Dede. *Asante Nsẹmfua Nkyerẹaseẹ Nwoma = Twi Dictionary*. Tema, Ghana: Aburuburo Nkosua Series, 2010.

Martinich, A. P. *Thomas Hobbes*. London: Macmillan Publishers Limited, 1996.

Matory, J. Lorand. "From 'Survival' to 'Dialogue': Analytic Tropes in the Study of African-Diaspora Cultural History." In *Transatlantic Caribbean: Dialogues of People, Practices, Ideas*, edited by Ingrid Kummels, Claudia Rauhut, Stefan Rinke, and Birte Timm, 33–55. London: Transcript-Verlag, 2014.

McFarlane, Ashley. *Re-Membering*. [Toronto, Canada]: [Unknown], 2011. DVD.

McFarlane, Milton C. *Cudjoe of Jamaica: Pioneer for Black Freedom in the New World*. Short Hills, NJ: R. Enslow, 1977.

McIver, Ann. "The Evolution of Belief Systems and Religious Practices Among the Maroons of Accompong, Jamaica." PhD diss., Occidental College, 1978.

Mintz, Sidney W. and Richard Price. *The Birth of African-American Culture: An Anthropological Perspective*. Boston: Beacon Press, 1992.

Montejo, Esteban and Miguel Barnet. *The Autobiography of a Runaway Slave*. New York: Meridian Books, 1969.

Ndlovu-Gatsheni, Sabelo J. *Coloniality of Power in Postcolonial Africa: Myths of Decolonization*. Dakar: Codesria, 2013.

Nisbett, Mario. "African Diasporic Traditional Symbols and Claims." In *Symbolism: An International Annual of Critical Aesthetics*, Volume 16, edited by Rüdiger Ahrens, Florian Kläger, Keith A. Sandiford and Klaus Stierstorfer, 117–138. Berlin, Germany: De Gruyter, 2016.

Obasare, Emmanuel Obaro. "Implications of Jamaican Maroon Understanding of Ancestors: An Interpretation." PhD diss., Fuller Theological Seminary, 2005.

Omi, Michael and Howard Winant. *Racial Formation in the United States: From the 1960s to the 1990s*. New York: Routledge, 1994.

Palmer, Colin A. "Defining and Studying the Modern African Diaspora." *Journal of Negro History* 85, no. 1/2 (2000): 27–32.

Palmié, Stephan. "Afterword: Descent and Alliance in Afro-Atlantic Anthropology." *Zeitschrift Für Ethnologie* 136, no. 2 (2011): 401–415.

Phillpotts, Karl and Marjorie Gammon. *Nanny*. Kingston: JAMAL Foundation, 1977.

Picart, Lennox O'Riley. *The Trelawny Maroons and Sir John Wentworth: The Struggle to Maintain Their Culture, 1796–1800*. [Fredericton, N.B.]: University of New Brunswick, 1993.

Pierre, Jemima. *The Predicament of Blackness: Postcolonial Ghana and the Politics of Race*. Chicago: The University of Chicago Press, 2013.

Pope, Polly. "A Maroon Settlement on St. Croix." *Negro History Bulletin* 35, no. 7 (1972): 153.

Prehay, Noel. "Introductory Remarks." Speech, Quao Day celebration, Scot's Hall, Jamaica, August 1, 2012.

——. "Welcome Remarks." Speech, Quao Day celebration, Charles Town, Jamaica, June 23, 2011.

Price, Richard. "Maroons in Anthropology." In *International Encyclopedia of the Social and Behavioral Sciences*, edited by Neil J. Smelser and Paul B. Baltes, 9253–9256. Oxford: Elsevier Science, 2001.

——, ed. *Maroon Societies: Rebel Slave Communities in the Americas*. Baltimore: Johns Hopkins University Press, 1996.

The Public Broadcasting Corporation of Jamaica. "Accompong Maroon Festival 2020." Accessed November 23, 2020. https://www.youtube.com/watch?v=XwJfLqz67Xs.

Queen Nanny of the Maroons. Facebook. Accessed December 29, 2020. https://www.facebook.com/Queen.Nanny/.

Reid, Hansley. Interview by author. Accompong Town, St. Elizabeth, Jamaica. December 21, 2011.

Reis, Joao Jose and Flavio dos Santos Gomes. "Quilombo: Brazilian Maroons during Slavery." *Cultural Survival Quarterly* 25, Issue 4 (2002): 19.

Renny, Robert. *An History of Jamaica: with Observations on the Climate, Scenery, Trade, Productions, Negroes, Slave Trade, Diseases of Europeans, Customs, Manners, and dispositions of the Inhabitants; to Which is Added, an Illustration of the Advantages, Which are Likely to Result from the Abolition of the Slave Trade*. London: Printed for J. Cawthorn, 1807.

Roberts, Neil. *Freedom as Marronage*. Chicago: The University of Chicago Press, 2015.

Robinson, Carey. *The Iron Thorn: The Defeat of the British by the Jamaican Maroons*. Kingston, Jamaica: Kingston Publishers, 1993.

Rowe, Garfield. Interview by author. Accompong Town, St. Elizabeth, Jamaica. January 10, 2013.

Rowe, Lawrence and Lance Ricketts. Interview by author. Accompong Town, St. Elizabeth, Jamaica. December 26, 2011.

Rowe, Mann O. Interview by an unknown interviewer. Undated. Interview T265, African Caribbean Institute of Jamaica, Kingston, Jamaica.

Rowe-Edwards, Norma. *My Father Said: A Story about the Accompong Maroons 1655–1738*. Riviera Beach, FL: Emerge Publishing Group, 2011.

Rugemer, Edward Bartlett. *Slave Law and the Politics of Resistance in the Early Atlantic World.* Cambridge, MA: Harvard University Press, 2018.

Schafer, Daniel Lee. "The Maroons of Jamaica: African Slave Rebels in the Caribbean." Ph.D. diss., University of Minnesota, 1975.

Schochet, Gordon J. "Thomas Hobbes on the Family and the State of Nature." *Political Science Quarterly* 82, no. 3 (Sept. 1967): 427–445.

Schwartz, Stuart B. *Slaves, Peasants, and Rebels: Reconsidering Brazilian Slavery.* Urbana: University of Illinois Press, 1992.

Scott, Darieck. *Extravagant Abjection: Blackness, Power, and Sexuality in the African American Literary Imagination.* New York: New York University Press, 2016.

Senior, Olive. *Encyclopedia of Jamaican Heritage.* St. Andrew, Jamaica: Twin Guinep, 2003.

Shepperson, George. "African Diaspora: Concept and Context." In *Global Dimensions of the African Diaspora*, edited by Joseph Harris, 41–50. Washington, DC: Howard University Press, 1982.

Sivapragasam, Michael. "After the Treaties: A Social, Economic and Demographic History of Maroon Society in Jamaica, 1739–1842." PhD diss., Southampton University, 2018.

Slack, Jennifer Daryl. "The Theory and Method of Articulation in Cultural Studies." In *Stuart Hall: Critical Dialogues in Cultural Studies*, edited by David Morley and Kuan-Hsing Chen, 112–127. New York: Taylor & Francis, 1996.

Sloane, Hans. *A Voyage to the Islands Madera, Barbados, Nieves, S. Christophers and Jamaica With the Natural History of the Herbs and Trees, Four-Footed Beasts, Fishes, Birds, Insects, Reptiles, &C. of the Last of Those Islands; to Which Is Prefix'd an Introduction, Wherein Is an Account of the Inhabitants, Air, Waters, Diseases, Trade, &C. of That Place, with Some Relations Concerning the Neighbouring Continent, and Islands of America. Illustrated with the Figures of the Things Describ'd, Which Have Not Been Heretofore Engraved; In Large Copper-Plates As Big As the Life. By Hans Sloane, M. D. Fellow of the College of Physicians and Secretary of the Royal-Society. In Two Volumes, Vol. I.* London: BM, 1707.

Smith, Hilary F. "Stakeholder Involvement in the Decision-Making for the Sustainable Development of the Cockpit Country, Jamaica." Master's thesis, State University of New York, Syracuse, 2009.

Smith, Robert Worthington. "The Legal Status of Jamaican Slaves Before the Anti-Slavery Movement." *The Journal of Negro History* 30, no. 3 (1945): 293–303.

Social Development Commission (SDC). *Community Profile: Accompong.* Kingston, Jamaica: SDC Research Department, 2011.

Sterling, Wallace. Interview by author. Moore Town, Portland, Jamaica. December 1, 2011.

Steward, J. "Interesting Notes on Jamaica." *The Atheneum*, November 15, 1823.

Tanna, Laura. *Jamaican Folk Tales and Oral Histories.* Kingston: Institute of Jamaica Publications, 1984.

Thompson, Alvin O. *Flight to Freedom African Runaways and Maroons in the Americas.* Kingston, Jamaica: University of West Indies Press, 2006.

Thompson, Willie. *Postmodernism and History*. Basingstoke, Hampshire: Palgrave Macmillan, 2004.

Tölölyan, Khachig. "Rethinking Diaspora(s): Stateless Power in the Transnational Moment." *Diaspora* 5, no. 1 (1996): 3–36.

The Trelawney Town Maroons of the Sovereign State of Accompong Constitution.

Tuelon, Alan. "Nanny—Maroon Chieftainess." *Caribbean Quarterly* 19, no. 4 (1973): 20–27.

Tyler, Imogen. *Revolting Subjects: Social Abjection and Resistance in Neoliberal Britain*. London: Zed Books Ltd, 2013.

The United Kingdom. The National Archives. CO 950/167, f. 1.

The United Kingdom. The National Archives. "H. A. Rowe to Colonial Office," [1938,] CO 950/167, f. 1.

Vansina, Jan. "Quilombos on São Thomé, or In Search of Original Sources." *History in Africa* 23 (1996): 453–459.

Warner-Lewis, Maureen. *Central Africa in the Caribbean: Transcending Time, Transforming Cultures*. Kingston, Jamaica: University of West Indies Press, 2003.

Weik, Terry. "The Archaeology of Maroon Societies in the Americas: Resistance, Cultural Continuity, and Transformation in the African Diaspora." *Historical Archaeology* 31, no. 2 (1997): 81–92.

Westergaard, Waldemar. *The Danish West Indies under Company Rule (1671–1754)*. New York: The Macmillan Company, 1917.

Williams, Ferron. Interview by author. Accompong Town, St. Elizabeth, Jamaica. January 7, 2012.

Williams, Joseph. *The Maroons of Jamaica*. Chestnut Hill, MA: Boston College Press, 1938.

Wilson, Kathleen. "The Performance of Freedom: Maroons and the Colonial Order in Eighteenth-Century Jamaica and the Atlantic Sound." *The William and Mary Quarterly* 66, no. 1 (2009): 64–86.

Wright, Martin-Luther. "Accompong Maroons of Jamaica." In *Maroon Heritage Archaeological, Ethnographic, and Historical Perspectives*, edited by E. Kofi Agorsah, 64–71. Barbados: Canoe Press, 1994.

Yelvington, Kevin A. "The Anthropology of Afro-Latin America and the Caribbean: Diasporic Dimensions Source." *Annual Review of Anthropology* 30 (2001): 227–260.

Zeleza, Paul Tiyambe. "The Challenges of Studying the African Diasporas." *African Sociological Review/Revue Africaine De Sociologie* 12, no. 2 (2008): 4–21.

Zips, Werner. *Black Rebels: African-Caribbean Freedom Fighters in Jamaica*. Princeton, NJ: Markus Wiener Publishers, 1999.

———. "Laws in Competition: Traditional Maroon Authorities Within Legal Pluralism in Jamaica." *Journal of Legal Pluralism and Unofficial Law* (1996): 279–306.

———. *Nanny's Asafo Warriors: The Jamaican Maroons' African Experience*. Kingston: Ian Randle, 2011.

———. "'We Are Landowners': Territorial Autonomy and Land Tenure in the Jamaican Maroon Community of Accompong." *Journal of Legal Pluralism and Unofficial Law* 40 (1998): 89–122.

Index

About Author

Mario O. Nisbett was educated at the University of the Virgin Islands (B.A.), Morgan State University (M.A.), and the University of California, Berkeley (M.A. & Ph.D.). He has taught at universities in the United States and Kenya. He is currently a Lecturer at the Centre for African and International Studies of the University of Cape Coast, Ghana. He is also senior researcher for the African Diaspora Institute of Cultural Exchange and Historical Research, Inc. His areas of research interest are global African studies, African/African diaspora histories, Pan-Africanism, and slavery and resistance.

www.ingramcontent.com/pod-product-compliance
Lightning Source LLC
Chambersburg PA
CBHW050520280326
41932CB00014B/2390
* 9 7 8 1 7 9 3 6 1 3 9 0 5 *